SEASON OF SERVICE

DAILY DEVOTIONALS AND SERVICE ACTIVITIES

Credits
We thank the following pastors that collaborated in this project

Ed Santana
Michaela Jeffery
Mike Pethel
Chuck Woods
Ralph Ringer
Bruce Trigg
Dr. Walter Castro
Rick Greeve
Alex Lampkin

This resource is brought to you for:

Churches-Groups-Individuals

by

Southern Union Ministerial Department and Pastors

Twitter: www.twitter.com/leadSU

Facebook: https://www.facebook.com/leadSU

Blog- www.leadsu.org

Slide Share: www.slideshare.net/RogerHernandez6

Youtube channel:
www.youtube.com/user/pastorRogerHernandez

L.E.A.D.
Leadership. Evangelism. Accountability. Diversity.

Thanks
to all the churches, people, small groups,
and organizations that work tirelessly
to make sure people in their communities
feel the hands and feet of Jesus.

How to use this resource

1. Purpose:
The idea behind this resource is to motivate, educate and release members to be the hands and feet of Jesus in our communities through a 40 Day Season of Service (SOS).

2. Daily Lesson:
Each lesson contains three parts:
See It- we always start with scripture. Don't be too quick to skip over it. Read it. Read it again. Internalize it. Believe it. Share it.
Obey It- This part shares a few principles to learn. They usually relate to the verse you just read. They are short, practical and biblical.
Share It- The last part of the lesson is where you turn your knowledge about service into action. Most of us are educated well above our level of obedience, so if you are only reading and not serving, this resource will be only partially successful. Each day you will have **3 options** of service activities for you to do **THAT** day. Pick one. (or more) There is also a list of **100 more** service projects that you, your church or small group can do during the SOS and beyond at the end of the book in **APPENDIX 1**.

3. Small Group Study
Included in this resource there are five small group lessons, enough for **one per week** for 40 days. These lessons can be studied in homes, workplaces, during Sabbath Services, or wherever God leads you. They are simple, easy and very practical.

4. Chronology
Start Day- first step is to start. It works best on a weekend day, but you can start it any day.
Daily 40- the next step is to complete the daily devotional/action step. If you miss a day, just go on to the next one. Chose "done" over "perfect."
Big Serve Weekend- Usually in the middle of the 40 days, there is a weekend that is reserved for larger projects. Check with your local leadership for dates.
Service Celebration- The last step is the final day of the 40 days. That Sabbath the ideal is that local civic leaders be invited and honored at the local church as well as informed about what the church has been doing. It's a high day!

Remember: Done over perfect!

A Special Message for Leaders
Dr. Walter Castro

Why do we serve?

Jesus said in Matthew 20:26-28, "Anyone wanting to be a leader among you must be your servant. And if you want to be right at the top, you must serve like a slave. Your attitude must be like my own, for I, the Messiah, did not come to be served, but to serve" (LB).

Then there is Luke 22:26, which says, "But among you, the one who serves you best will be your leader."

These two verses are the foundation for Christian leadership. Jesus said the exact opposite of what the world says about what a real leader is. In the world, you build a pyramid and you climb to the top. But Jesus said, "No, he who serves best leads best."

Servant-hood is leadership. The better you serve, the more God raises you up to leadership.

Leadership is not a matter of getting people to serve your interests. Leadership is a matter of serving the best interests of others. Jesus said, "If you want to be great, you learn to be the servant of all."

"The servant-leader is servant first... It begins with the natural feeling that one wants to serve, to serve first. Then conscious choice brings one to aspire to lead. That person is sharply different from one who is leader first, perhaps because of the need to assuage an unusual power drive or to acquire material possessions... The leader-first and the servant-first are two extreme types. Between them there are shadings and blends that are part of the infinite variety of human nature.

"The difference manifests itself in the care taken by the servant-first to make sure that other people's highest priority needs are being served. The best test, and difficult to administer, is: Do those served grow as persons? Do they, while being served, become healthier, wiser, freer, more autonomous, more likely themselves to become servants? And, what is the effect on the least privileged in society? Will they benefit or at least not be further deprived?" (The Servant as Leader, an essay that he first published in 1970.)

Many people believe great leaders are charismatic, have a commanding presence, are visionary and educated at elite schools. Not necessarily. Here are four reasons why we serve:

1. **We were designed to serve.** Ephesians 2:10 says, "It is God Himself who has made us what we are and given us new lives from Christ Jesus; and long ages ago He planned that we should spend these lives in helping others." Even before you were born, God planned a life of service for you.

One reason why so many people are miserable today is because they've missed the point of life. As I serve others, my own needs are met, and as I give my life away, I find it. You were created for service.

2. We serve God by serving others. Colossians 3:23-24 says, "Whatever you do, work at it with all your heart as working for the Lord and not for men. It is the Lord you are serving." No matter what you're doing, who are you doing it for? You're doing it for the Lord. In Matthew 25:40, Jesus said, "What you have done for the humblest of My brothers you have done for Me." He states it positively: "If you feed and clothe others, then you feed and clothe Me. If you haven't fed and clothed others, you haven't fed and clothed Me."

3. It's the best use of our lives. I Corinthians 15:58 says, "Keep busy always in your work for the Lord, since you know that nothing you do in the Lord's service is ever useless." When I go home and play with my kids, that's as important a service as preparing a sermon. When I take out the garbage so my wife can go do something else, that's just as significant service as when I'm speaking to a crowd, because it all counts in God's eyes.

4. Serving will be rewarded for eternity. John 12:26, Jesus said, "My Father will honor the ones who serve Me." And in Matthew 25:21, He says, "Well done, good and faithful servants. You've been faithful in a few things. I'll put you in charge of many things. Come and share your master's happiness." This life is a test. You're being tested, and God is seeing what kind of faithfulness you have. It's worth the effort!

The Hebrew word for leader is "nagiyd." It pictures a person under authority who fulfills the wishes of that authority. God wants leaders who will listen to His will and execute it faithfully with divinely appointed authority. The related Greek word for leadership is "diakonia." This literally means serving at tables.

Servant-leadership is not simply doing menial tasks, nor does it serve as a strategy to satisfy the leaders own needs. Servant-leaders invest themselves in enabling others to do their best. They are willing to do humble tasks, but they always have in mind a larger vision. Servant-leaders must first of all please God.

As you begin the **S.O.S.**, remember why we do this: We are servant leaders.

CONTENTS

DAILY DEVOTIONALS AND SERVICE ACTIVITIES - PART I 9
- FREEDOM 10
- RISK 11
- FEAR 12
- OUT 13
- VALUE 14
- SERVICE 15
- INTERRUPTION 16
- MORE 17
- FORGIVING 18
- PHARISEES 19
- RETURN 20
- SACRIFICE 21
- STORMS 22
- CRITICS 23
- BROTHER 24
- PROGRAMS 25
- CAVE 26
- FRIENDS 27
- HIM 28
- VISION 29
- GIVING 30
- SERVING 31
- BEYOND 32
- BLESSING 33
- GRACE 34
- TODAY 35
- TIMELY 36
- POOR 37
- LIGHT 38
- OBEDIENCE 39
- EXPECT 40
- COACH 41
- CREATE 42
- WORDS 43
- UNITY 44
- GUESTS 45
- LOVE 46
- IMPACT 47
- INVITATION 48
- CHANGE 49
- FINAL THOUGHS 50

100+ COMMUNITY SERVANT EVANGELISM IDEAS FOR YOUR CHURCH - APPENDIX 1 51

SMALL GROUP LESSONS - PART II 64
- THE NEED TO SERVE 65
- THE TIME TO SERVE 66
- LIFE IS NOT A SELF-SERVICE 67
- THE COST OF SERVICE 68
- OPEN HAND CHRISTIANS 69

PART I

DAILY DEVOTIONALS AND SERVICE ACTIVITIES

FREEDOM

PART I — DAY 1

SEE IT
Isaiah 61:1: "The Spirit of the Sovereign LORD is on me, because the LORD has anointed me to proclaim good news to the poor. He has sent me to bind up the brokenhearted, to proclaim freedom for the captives and release from darkness for the prisoners...."

OBEY IT
We can learn three lessons from today's text.
1. Each of us struggles with overcoming something. Drugs, alcohol, pornography, gossip, constant bad moods, workaholism, inappropriate sex, irritability, materialism, legalism. This is by no means an exhaustive list, but it does tell us about the reality of being human. We're bad when we're born, and we get worse. The first step to bein g free is recognize what enslaves us. Offer a prayer right now and confess your weakness before God. As you go through your day give grace to those who are struggling. Remember the grace God has given you.
2. All can be set free.
Whatever your question, God has an answer. Whatever your need, God has the solution. Whatever your wound, God has the cure. Freedom is not only for the few and the privileged, but for everyone—for you. Do you believe that? This helps us not to discount anyone, no matter how deep their addiction or dysfunction. **ALL** can be set free. All.
3. Freedom is a process. The Bible tells us that it may take some time from the time you are declared free (justification) to the moment you start to experience the results (sanctification). It's like walking on dry land after being in a boat. For a while you still feel like you're at sea, though you're really on land. It's a very real feeling, though temporary. The fact that you may still feel the effects of the chains around your ankles doesn't mean that they are not gone. You're now free. Believe it. This helps us be patient with others. We don't compare ourselves with our fellow travelers, or criticize them because they sin differently than us. We are on a journey, let's encourage each other on the way.

SHARE IT
You probably know people who are battling an addiction. Connect with them today and let them know that you are available to talk or pray with or for them.

My Prayer Today: For people that struggle with addictions
1. Pray that God will break the chains of addiction.
2. Pray that those afflicted will believe they can be free.

My Thoughts _____

_____

PART I DAY 2

RISK

SEE IT

Mathew 9:1 Jesus climbed into a boat and went back across the lake to his own town. [2] Some people brought to him a paralyzed man on a mat. Seeing their faith, Jesus said to the paralyzed man, "Be encouraged, my child! Your sins are forgiven." [3] But some of the teachers of religious law said to themselves, "That's blasphemy! Does he think he's God?"

OBEY IT

Jamil is a risk taker. He is a gymnastics expert. He trusts that when he does the flips and jumps, someone will not let him hit his head on the cement floor. That is risk. That is faith. Mathew 9 shows several people taking a risk that was blessed by God. The four friends that took a risk and opened the ceiling in a house that was not their own. Result? Healing. Mathew took a risk when he was called and left everything on the table. Literally. Result? Growth. The woman who suffered from a non-stop menstruation took a risk and touched His garment. Result? Miracle. The two blind men took a risk and yelled incessantly when others told them to be quiet. Result? Sight. Do you see a pattern here? What can we learn from these stories?

1. Helping people is risky. I wonder what the owner of the house thought when he saw a hole in his roof. The four friends understood that Jesus didn't come to preserve structures, he came to save souls. So they made the hole. The question becomes not whether something is risky, but whether it's biblical and therefore worth it.

2. Criticism follows risk. Not everyone will appreciate or support your choice to minister on behalf of God. Sometimes even those closest to you will be your harshest critics. It is interesting that the Pharisees were never seen helping anyone, yet criticized anyone who tried to. Don't be dissuaded by criticism. It is the sandpaper God uses to polish his work of art.

3. God honors God honoring risks. That is a fact. The question becomes: What God honoring risk are you taking today?

SHARE IT

Action steps for today:
1. Instead of just thinking it, compliment someone publicly. 2. Give a sad looking stranger a happy music DC or card. 3. Ask someone "how are you?" Mean it. Listen to them.

My Prayer Today:
The only thing that consistently brings us close to God is taking a risk, because it forces you to seek God's intervention. Take a God honoring risk today and pray: "God help me be bold, despite of my fears."

My Thoughts _____

FEAR

**PART I
DAY 3**

SEE IT
Mathew 25:24 "Then the servant with the one bag of silver came and said, 'Master, I knew you were a harsh man, harvesting crops you didn't plant and gathering crops you didn't cultivate. [25] **I was afraid** I would lose your money, so I hid it in the earth. Look, here is your money back.'

OBEY IT
What would you do if you knew failure was not possible? Today, take some time to read Matthew 25. It's a great chapter. One of the stories it shares is about three people that were given some money. Two invested it and increased their earnings, one did not. He said something very revealing: "I was afraid". Fear paralyzed him. It can do the same to us too. Here are some lessons from that passage:
1. Our perception of who God is directly affects our tolerance for risk. If we see a God who is mad, angry, and concentrate on his judgment while neglecting his grace, our service for him decreases. That reality directly affects the people around us, because our gifts were made to bless others, not to be hoarded and hidden.
2. If God has given you gifts he expects a return investment. In case you forgot, he was the one who gave you the 5,2, or 1 talents you have in the first place. You didn't get those talents on your own to begin with!
3. God has not called you to be someone you are not. If you are a 2 talent person, he does not want you to act like a 5 talent. Or a 1 talent. He doesn't want us to be **everything** or do **everything** but he does want us to do *something*. Like serving someone else with our 5, 2 or 1 talents. Help. Not hide.

SHARE IT
Today do this:
1. Fill an expired or about to expire parking meter.
2. Leave some extra money in the vending machine.
3. Buy a little extra grocery for the local food bank.

My Prayer Today:
Something is going to happen today that will test your faith. Walk through it without fear. Pray this: "God, help me be ready to try something new."

My Thoughts _____

_____

**PART I
DAY 4**

OUT

SEE IT
Luke 1:7 They had no children because Elizabeth was unable to conceive, and they were both very old.

OBEY IT
One of the most rewarding things I remember as a parent is seeing my kids play organized baseball (Jonas) and softball (Vanessa). They were athletically gifted but they also sometimes struck out. Strike three means you sit. You failed. You're **out**! If you notice in today's text which is part of a larger story of a miracle, God uses people and situations that are less than ideal, downright difficult and bordering on impossible. Elizabeth and Zechariah had three strikes against them that are also three lessons:
1. Old (well, you know what that means...) God uses people that are past their prime.
2. Unfertile (could not conceive) God uses people that are working with impossibilities.
3. Unbelief (he didn't believe it was possible) God uses people that don't have perfect faith.

God took a package of nothing, and made them parents. He took a stutterer and made him a leader. He took an easy woman and made her an example of virtue. Surely he can use you. Surely you are not **out**. Remember that:

> "God takes men as they are... They are not chosen because they are perfect, but notwithstanding their imperfections, that through the knowledge and practice of the truth, through the grace of Christ, they may become transformed into His image."
> Desire of Ages, p. 294

SHARE IT
Pick one today:
1. Prepare a meal for a homeless person.
2. Smile more than usual. :)
3. Call your mother or family member to tell them "I love you."

My Prayer Today:
You probably have deficiencies in an area. God, I believe can use you in spite of _____. Lord, thanks for choosing me. I wow to keep hitting. Keep serving.

My Thoughts _____

_____

VALUE

**PART I
DAY 5**

SEE IT
Mark 5:13 So Jesus gave them permission. The evil spirits came out of the man and entered the pigs, and the entire herd of about 2,000 pigs plunged down the steep hillside into the lake and drowned in the water.

OBEY IT
We can learn three lessons from today's text.
This story always gets to me. Here is this guy who is terrorizing the community. He goes to Grandma's grave, pulls her out and sleeps in her grave. Jesus comes in and takes not one or one hundred but 2,000 demons out from him. Think about that. 2,000 demons. How does it feel to be inhabited by 2,000 demons? Here are some lessons we can learn:

1. The people see the man healed but they care more for the pigs than the person. Same thing happens today. We use people and love things. Many just care about what people can do for us. Its pigs over people all over again.

2. Anyone can be restored. This man had issues with his family, finances, friends, relationships, health, and more importantly his spirituality. No one is so far, God can't reach. In High School I had a friend who had one ear missing. Correa was his last name. People dismissed him, made fun of him. I invited him to spend the weekend with me. Made his year. With all the dumb stuff I did in high school, this was one good thing I remember. One act of love can make a person's day.

3. Let's love people, not pigs. We have it backwards sometimes. We use people and love things. Service helps us understand that when Jesus comes back, he won't be coming for your church pews, the keys to the church kitchen or care for the color of the church walls. People are a higher value. If we need to choose, let's choose people.

SHARE IT
1. Write a handwritten note (not an email or text) for someone people ignore.
2. Knit a beanie or blanket or buy one for a homeless person.
3. Put change in the washer/dryer for the next person.

My Prayer Today:
Jesus, help me love people over possessions and help me demonstrate that I care about others through my acts of service today.

My Thoughts _____

_____

PART I DAY 6

SERVICE

SEE IT

"There is need of coming close to the people by personal effort. If less time were given to sermonizing, and more time were spent in personal ministry, greater results would be seen. The **poor** are to be relieved, the **sick** cared for, the **sorrowing** and the bereaved comforted, the **ignorant** instructed, the **inexperienced** counseled. We are to weep with those that weep, and rejoice with those that rejoice. Accompanied by the power of persuasion, the power of prayer, the power of the love of God, **this work will not, cannot, be without fruit.**" **(Ministry of Healing 143-144)**

OBEY IT

This quote bundles evangelism and service. Here are some principles to remember:

1. A service lifestyle is part of a divine expectation. It would be helpful to understand that when standing before our maker, instead of asking us to recite the eschatological timeline, God asks "what did you do about my children that needed help?" Mathew 25:34-36

2. A service lifestyle takes us out of our comfort zone. It's more than outreach, its reaching out. Even to those who don't look, believe, speak, or act like us. That includes our enemies! Mathew 5:46-48

3. A service lifestyle breaks down barriers. It's all about love, and love can indeed "conquer all". When we express love, we break down pre-conceived concepts about the church and God. Most people, when they think about church, associate it more with asking for things than giving you things. Service goes a long way to change that perception.

SHARE IT

Remember, there are **37** recorded miracles of Jesus in the New Testament. There is **one** written sermon of Jesus (Mat. 5-7). Remember the initial quote? "If less time were given to sermonizing, and more time were spent in personal ministry, greater results would be seen". **(Ministry of Healing, 143)**

My Prayer Today:
"Lord, help me to preach more with my actions than what I do with my verbs."

My Thoughts _____

_____

◆ INTERRUPTION ◆

SEE IT ◆
Isaiah 41:4 "I am the only God and I keep under control everything that happens in this world. I have existed from the beginning, and will exist until the end. "

OBEY IT ◆
I was very engaged with an article that I was writing. Words were flowing, thoughts were coming. I was "in the zone". Then it happened. My son came into the room and asked me if we could play some basketball. Interruption! Most of us see interruptions as negative occurrences that come to disturb our carefully crafted calendar, but it need not be so. Here are three principles to make interruptions your ally:

1. They may seem like interruptions to you, but they were on God's calendar.
We define interruptions as "an encounter or event that was not planned." If we look at the life of Jesus as an example, we can see his reaction to interruptions. Jesus blessed children, resurrected the dead, healed the sick, all outside of the programmed schedule for that day. That interruption you are experiencing might be God's chance to perform a miracle.

2. Submit your calendar to God, which involves surrendering control of yours.
Someone said that if you want to make God smile tell him your final/definite plans. Submit your calendar to God. You're not in the driver's seat, and Jesus is not your co-pilot. Expect interruptions to come into your life today.

3. Instead of thinking how the interruption affects you, think about how it helps others.
God is calling you to pause for a moment today, and instead of seeing the interruption like a stone in your shoe, think about how your help will be a blessing to the person who does not even have shoes. We don't use people to achieve our dreams, we help others discover theirs and help them to become reality. Remember that **Often our plans fail that God's plans for us may succeed.** *Help in Daily Living*, p. 6

SHARE IT ◆
1. Call someone you haven't talked to in a while. 2. Give someone a flower ...or a dozen.
3. Offer someone else your spot on the bus/train/line.

My Prayer Today:
God, direct my calendar today. Take over my schedule and help me take advantage of those "God appointments" Make interruptions my ally today. Amen.
My Thoughts _____

PART I DAY 8

MORE

SEE IT

Mark 10: 28 Then Peter began to speak up. "We've given up everything to follow you," he said. ²⁹ "Yes," Jesus replied, "and I assure you that everyone who has given up **house or brothers or sisters or mother or father or children or property,** for my sake and for the Good News, ³⁰ will receive now in return a **hundred times** as many houses, brothers, sisters, mothers, children, and property—along with persecution. And in the world to come that person will have eternal life. ³¹ But many who are the greatest now will be least important then, and those who seem least important now will be the greatest then."

OBEY IT

One of the questions we ask ourselves as we follow Christ is this: **Is it worth it?** When Jesus calls us to serve others, it involves giving up some things we love. Peter asked Jesus about three things he gave up to follow Jesus:
1. **House-** the security of knowing where you will live.
2. **Family-** the closeness of the people you love.
3. **Property-** the financial security that comes with property.

If you are willing to give up those things, bigger blessings will come, none bigger than eternal life. That is our real motivation. All the other accolades, properties and possessions will be done away when Jesus comes back. Therefore, salvation of ourselves and others is paramount. We don't just serve because we want people to be better off. We serve because we want people to be saved. Remember that:

> "Our heavenly Father has a thousand ways to provide
> for us of which we know nothing. Those who accept the one principle
> of making the service of God supreme will find perplexities vanish
> and a plain path before their feet.
> Help in Daily Living, p. 13

SHARE IT
1. Make some baked goods for your neighbor(s).
2. Hug your loved ones for no particular reason.
3. Make breakfast for your spouse or roommate.

My Prayer Today:
Lord, help me look past the temporary inconveniences in this life and remember the eternal consequence of serving you and others. Amen.

My Thoughts _____

FORGIVING

**PART I
DAY 9**

SEE IT
Mark 11:25 when you are praying, first forgive anyone you are holding a grudge against, so that your Father in heaven will forgive your sins, too.

OBEY IT
I remember it well. I heard someone was talking bad about my dad. I was in high school. It bothered me all day. I Could not get it out of my head, so I let it dictate what I would do. After school, I went up to him and punched him. Very dumb in my part. Today he is my Facebook friend, has forgiven me, and I look back on my decision with regret. He truly forgave my aggression. Jesus has asked us to serve everyone and that includes people we don't particularly get along with. Why is it important to forgive and serve those who have hurt us? The truth is this: what we resent we reflect. Be careful about lack of forgiveness in three areas:
1. What others have done to you intentionally. Forgive and serve.
2. What you have done to yourself. Forgive and serve.
3. What "powers that be" have done to you. Forgive and serve.

Forgiveness does not always mean re-establishment of relationship, especially if there is emotional or physical harm. It does mean loving them and helping them regardless. Who do you need to forgive today? Who can you show you have forgiving by paying good for evil through service?

SHARE IT
1. Practice patience.
2. Refrain from gossiping; speak well of others.
3. Act as if the glass was half full.

My Prayer Today:
Lord, I know forgiveness is not easy, but it's necessary. Help me to serve people I don't particularly like or agree with today. Amen.

My Thoughts _____

_____

**PART I
DAY 10**

PHARISEES

SEE IT

Mark 12:38 Jesus also taught: "Beware of these teachers of religious law! For they like to parade around in flowing robes and receive respectful greetings as they walk in the marketplaces. [39] And how they love the seats of honor in the synagogues and the head table at banquets. [40] Yet they shamelessly cheat widows out of their property and then pretend to be pious by making long prayers in public. Because of this, they will be more severely punished."

OBEY IT

It is clear from scripture that God not only cares that we serve others, but he cares why we serve others. The spirit of a Pharisee looks to help others when it's convenient for their own purposes. There are three problems with Pharisees:

1. They love for people to recognize THEM.
In reality all we do should point to something greater than us: Jesus. Pharisees will not waste a second before telling you what they are doing. When you serve, tell others about how good God is, not how much you did.

2. They care more for less important things.
The text says that Pharisees care for opinion of people yet forget to help the needy. Is that the reality in your life? Your congregation? Your family? Do you care more for people that are far from God than your group of friends from church? Usually in churches, the problem is not that we are not friendly, it's that we are friendly only with ourselves. Decide to change that!

3. Their personal life is a mess.
Publicly they front. Privately they steal. I've yet to meet a Pharisee that did not have private struggles that manifested themselves publicly, later. We usually criticize to deflect attention to our own dysfunctions. The best way to deal with out private struggles is to accept and extend grace. Especially to those we deem not worthy to receive it.

SHARE IT

1. Compliment a stranger sincerely.
2. Run an errand for someone.
3. Give something awesome away on craigslist.

My Prayer Today:
Lord, help me care for the important things. To love you and care for your children. Help me leave the accolades for others. Amen

My Thoughts
___

RETURN

PART I DAY 11

SEE IT

Mark 13:34 "The coming of the Son of Man can be illustrated by the story of a man going on a long trip. When he left home, he gave each of his slaves instructions about the work they were to do, and he told the gatekeeper to watch for his return. [35] You, too, must keep watch! For you don't know when the master of the household will return—in the evening, at midnight, before dawn, or at daybreak. [36] Don't let him find you sleeping when he arrives without warning. [37] I say to you what I say to everyone: Watch for him!"

OBEY IT

Jesus is coming back. That phrase causes fear in some, happiness in others and a yawn in others. Today's text encourages us to do three things:

1. Stay occupied. Some people in our churches dedicate their attention to last day conspiracies. Jesus says, "stay busy". It's not your job to figure when it will happen, but to understand that it will happen. .

2. Stay alert. It can happen anytime. If you noticed the text says that he will come at night, which is a time otherwise reserved for sleeping (evening, midnight, before dawn). The temptation is to relax. Don't. Instead, occupy, until he comes. Watch and pray.

3. Stay expectant. It can happen this year. It can happen in 10 years. The expectation keeps our hope alive and that hope provides strength in the middle of the trials.

My dad traveled sometimes. When he would come home to our home in Cayey, PR, I remember one time he brought me a watch from his trip. It came in a little box, and I was so thankful and happy when I received it. I can just think of the day when my heavenly father returns. Not with a box, but with my salvation in his hands.

SHARE IT

1. Send a friend an old photo and recall old times.
2. Send a random person in the phone book a small gift.
3. Send your sibling or family member or co-worker a small gift anonymously.

My Prayer Today:
Lord, I look forward to your coming. Not with fear or a yawn but with expectation and hope. Help me stay busy helping others in the meanwhile. Amen.

My Thoughts _____

_____

⬥ SACRIFICE ⬥

SEE IT
Mark 14:64 "Guilty!" they all cried. "He deserves to die!" ⁶⁵ Then some of them began to spit at him, and they blindfolded him and beat him with their fists. "Prophesy to us," they jeered. And the guards slapped him as they took him away.

OBEY IT
The gospel of Mark is pretty graphic when talking about Jesus' last days. He talks about the pain and suffering Jesus was put trough. It's easy to look at what Jesus went through and shake our heads with disgust. How could they? Why would they? But the truth is: I did this. I spit on Jesus. I beat him up. I nailed him, hit him, and killed him. That is the truth of the gospel. Jesus went willingly to a death caused by my lying, evil desires, pride, sin. He took my punishment, I took his glory. And there is NOTHING I could ever do to repay him. Therefore we need to ask ourselves the following three questions:
1. Why would he? One word: love. Love for us kept him from coming down from the cross. Is it possible that in the midst of all out theological education, religious knowledge and prophetic understanding we sometimes neglect the reason for our salvation, i/e the cross? Without it, everything else becomes either harder or complicated.
2. How could we? I don't believe it's possible to look at his sacrifice and be unwilling to sacrifice ourselves. When we don't, we won't. Take a bit of time today to reflect on the cross. Let that be your motivation for service. He died for us. That's why we sing. That's why we worship. That's why we serve.
3. When will we? Now that we understand what it means to be saved by grace, through faith, plus nothing, period, we need to act on it. It would be hypocritical to expect grace from God and extend law to others. Let's act with love.

SHARE IT
1. Spend time with the elderly.
2. Share your secret recipe with a friend.
3. Write a letter of appreciation.

My Prayer Today:
Jesus, today I just want to thank you. Don't want to ask for anything, just want to say thank you.

My Thoughts _____

_____

STORMS

PART I
DAY 13

SEE IT

Mark 4:38 Jesus was sleeping at the back of the boat with his head on a cushion. The disciples woke him up, shouting, "Teacher, don't you care that we're going to drown?" [39] When Jesus woke up, he rebuked the wind and said to the waves, "Silence! Be still!" Suddenly the wind stopped, and there was a great calm. [40] Then he asked them, "Why are you afraid? Do you still have no faith?"

OBEY IT

A while back, a pretty nasty storm griped the south. Storms come in all shapes and sizes to our lives:
A cancer diagnosis.
A breakup in a family.
A habit that leads to a bad choice that leads to a negative consequence.
A lack of _____.

Storms do three things.
1. Storms reveal what you think about Jesus. The disciples thought Jesus didn't care. We do the same sometimes. We blame Him for the bad that happens and attribute the good to talent or good luck.
2. Storms reveal who is really in control. We are not. He is.
3. Storms reveal the power of Jesus. He calmed their storm. He can calm yours.

There are people around you who are in the midst of storms. People that would otherwise not be interested in spiritual things are more open in the middle of a crisis. You may be able to share this thought with them.

SHARE IT

1. Introduce yourself to someone you always see around.
2. Anonymously send a friend in need some cash.
3. Invite someone who is alone over for dinner.

My Prayer Today:
Help me Father, to see with your eyes the people around me that are in the midst of a storm and provide support and guidance through your Holy Spirit and your peace. Amen

My Thoughts _____

_____

**PART I
DAY 14**

CRITICS

SEE IT

Mathew 16:16 To what can I compare this generation? It is like children playing a game in the public square. They complain to their friends, ¹⁷ 'We played wedding songs, and you didn't dance, so we played funeral songs, and you didn't mourn.' ¹⁸ For John didn't spend his time eating and drinking, and you say, 'He's possessed by a demon.' ¹⁹ The Son of Man, on the other hand, feasts and drinks, and you say, 'He's a glutton and a drunkard, and a **friend of tax collectors and other sinners!**' But wisdom is shown to be right by its results."

OBEY IT

If you serve people, you will surely be criticized. In fact, if you are intentional and persistent in reaching the ones God misses the most, you will suffer a case of friendly fire. The Pharisees criticized Jesus and found Him "guilty by association". But as Andy Stanley reminds us, "If Jesus feared guilt by association, he would have stayed in heaven." When you are criticized remember these three principles:
1. People that always complain are like children. If you listen to them you are in reality letting kids rule your life. Do you really want that?
2. No matter what Jesus did, people always criticized. So go ahead and be the person God is calling you to be. You will be happier, healthier and at the end more satisfied.
3. Results will show the truth. Mathew 16:19 says the "wisdom is shown by results" This means: let your results talk for themselves, DON'T DEFEND YOURSELF TO PEOPLE. Stop living your life based on others opinions.

SHARE IT

1. Leave some extra stamps at the post office for the next costumer.
2. Donate an hour of your professional services.
3. Leave chocolate for your co-worker.

My Prayer Today:
Lord, help me be the person you called me to be, regardless of opposition, criticism or gossip. Amen.

My Thoughts _____

_____

BROTHER

PART I
DAY 15

SEE IT
Luke 15:11 To illustrate the point further, Jesus told them this story: "A man had two sons. ¹² The younger son told his father, 'I want my share of your estate now before you die.' So his father agreed to divide his wealth between his sons. ¹³ "A few days later this younger son packed all his belongings and moved to a distant land, and there he wasted all his money in wild living.

OBEY IT
Based on the parable of the prodigal son, let's look at three things the **older brother did not do:**

1. He did not stop his brother from leaving.
Nowhere in the story do you see the younger brother pleading/talking/interceding with his younger sibling to get him to stay. He never calls him brother. Not once. He calls him names, he calls him "your son" but he never calls him brother. Instead let's say: you may end up leaving, but you are someone I am willing to fight for.

2. He did not search for him while he was gone.
It is interesting that the older brother was pretty specific about the lifestyle that his brother was leading, which begs the question: How did he know? It's so much easier to judge from afar, than it is to get in the pig pen and rescue the lost. Let's remember that lost people matter to God and that it's pretty hard to embrace someone you are pointing at.

3. He did not rejoice when he came back.
Here is the clincher. The bible says that the older, holier brother "**came near**" to the house. Interesting terminology. What he did not realize is that he too was far from the house. He too needed grace. He needed to understand that maybe he wasn't *as bad*, but he was *bad enough*.
"These who have erred need pity, they need help, they need sympathy. They suffer in their feelings and are frequently desponding and discouraged. Above everything else, they need **free forgiveness." (3Tp.128)**

SHARE IT
1. Collect clothes to take to a local shelter.
2. Stop to have a conversation with a homeless person.
3. Give an inspiring book to a struggling friend.

My Prayer Today:
Father, help me fight for them, search for them and rejoice with them. Amen.

My Thoughts _____

_____

SEASON OF SERVICE

**PART I
DAY 16**

⟡ **PROGRAMS** ⟡

SEE IT
Luke 19:10 For the Son of Man came to seek and save those who are lost."

OBEY IT
Today's devotional thought is intentionally written for leaders. The ones that make programs run. We don't need any *"just because programs"*. Just because programs are those we do **"just because" with no missional component.** Remember these three things:

1. Have a compelling vision to reach the lost.
You want to reach the city? What does that mean? Did you know that reaching the city means that sinners from said city will be coming to YOUR church, sitting next to YOUR daughter, and going to YOUR church picnic with their earrings, cigarette smell (not Marlboro, either) and (gasp) real chicken? The truth is that many times "we are afraid of the people we claim we want to reach. [1] We can't say: "we want to grow, but we don't want to do much."

2. Have the guts to lead in your sphere of influence.
If this is a God given vision, you must proceed. Make sure you are not changing doctrine, biblical principles, and the 10 commandments. Fierce, determined, hurtful opposition is a given. The devil hates evangelism. You will see how much when you become missional.

3. Bring alignment to the vision.
There can't be competing visions. Stay away from FUBU church. For us, by us, and the end of the day, it's just us. That's not what God had in mind when he created the church and launched it. Remember who we are doing it for: Jesus. Them. Us. In that order.

SHARE IT
1. Pay for the person behind you at the drive-thru.
2. Buy dessert for someone eating out alone
3. Pick up the tab for a random table at a restaurant.

My Prayer Today:
Father, help me grasp your passion to reach our community with your truth and love. Help me do what furthers your plan to seek and save. Amen.
My Thoughts _____

_____

---

[1]Williams, Zach (2013-12-04). Transitioning the Church: Leading the Established Church to Reach the Unchurched (Kindle Location 765). Rainer Publishing. Kindle Edition.

CAVE

PART I
DAY 17

SEE IT
1 Samuel 22:1 So David left Gath and escaped to the cave of Adullam. Soon his brothers and all his other relatives joined him there. ² Then others began coming—men who were in trouble or in debt or who were just discontented—until David was the captain of about 400 men.

OBEY IT
How can we serve others, when our own private life is falling apart? Today's text shows us a future king, living in a cave with many problems in his hands. Here are three principles that have helped me, especially when having a cave experience:

1. Learn from it. Never waste a cave experience.
One of the most practical ways bad experiences have prepared me is when I see people struggling with some of the same issues I went through, and being able to tell them: It's going to be alright. Never waste a cave experience. Grow from it. Learn from it. Help others after you are done with it.

2. Serve your way out. Never get comfortable in the cave.
David "became the leader" of about 400 people in the cave. He understood that he must lead the ones you have, not the ones you want to have. Leaders are thermostats. They set the temperature in the room. They do not let circumstances determine effort. They give their best, do their best, where they are.

3. Look for people God sends your way. Never go at it alone.
Life is difficult. When you are in the midst of the chaos, God will always send someone to help you through it. Sometimes we are so focused on what's going on that we ignore mentors and try to go at it alone. Mentors will give you perspective, encouragement and accountability.

SHARE IT
1. Mentor local youth.
2. Put $10 on a random gas pump.
3. Buy flowers for the cashier at the grocery store.

My Prayer Today:
Father, help me understand that I can still be of service to you, even though my conditions are not perfect. Help me serve you in this "cave". Amen.

My Thoughts _____

_____

PART I DAY 18

FRIENDS

SEE IT
At creation our heavenly Father made every provision for our happiness, He included friends as a key ingredient. The Lord God said, "It is not good that the man should be alone," Genesis 2:18. God gave man the animal creation for low level companionship. This relationship describes superior to inferior. Likewise, God gave man other humans for companionship thus this represents mutual social relationships.

OBEY IT
The word "friend" appears in the Bible (King James) 53 times. Friendly appears 3 times. Friends appear 49 times. Friendship appears twice. As a quick reference word study, the Old Testament the word for friend is reya in Proverbs 18:24 which means brother, associate, companion, friend, or neighbor. In the New Testament, the Greek terms used most include philos or "friend". Let's consider three things about friends.

1. Purpose of Friends
Today's generation seem to posses the habit of being ant-social. They don't trust anybody, so they live guarded lives. Being alone is not negative, but being a lone-ranger without friends as support becomes alarming. We're here on this planet not only to make something of ourselves, but also leave our mark in the most memorable manner. It's our privilege to touch those around us with our friendship and support. Each of us can help change our friends lives, help them bounce back from the lowest of times, and help them learn about the love of God. "A friend loves at all times...," Proverbs 17:17.

2. Practice of Friends
Proverbs 27:17 says, "iron sharpens iron as a friend sharpens a friend." Someone said there are three types of friends. First, mentor friend teaches, counsels, or disciples. Second, mentee friend is taught, counseled, or discipled. Third, mutual friends are not mentored, but closely aligned on same level balancing the natural flow of giving and receiving between genuine friends. As we meet new people and expand our social circles, we'll encounter individuals from all walks of life with stories to tell and personalities to share. People help us in more ways than we can imagine, but mostly they help us to broaden our outlook on life.

3. Power of Friends
One of my favorite story tells the story of a man journeying on a winter's day through deep drifts of snow became benumb by the cold which was freezing his vital powers. "Nearly chilled to death, and about to give up the struggle for life heard the moans of a fellow traveler who was perishing in the cold. Sympathy aroused, determined to rescue the man, he raised the suffer to his feet, bore him through the very drifts he thought he could never get through alone. Traveling to a place of safety, the truth flashed home to him that in saving his neighbor he saved himself." Welfare Ministry p. 305. Friends possess a power to change lives as well as the world around them.

SHARE IT
1. Clean up your area at work, and a common one as well.
2. Pick up trash.
3. Pay for the drink, meal, or toll of the person behind you.

My Prayer Today:
Father, help me be loving in my relationships, and help me serve even those I do not get along with. Amen.

My Thoughts _____

HIM

PART I
DAY 19

SEE IT
Mark 3:13 Jesus went up on a mountainside. He called for certain people to come to him, and they came. ¹⁴ He appointed 12 of them and called them apostles. From that time on they would be with him. He would also send them out to preach. ¹⁵ They would have authority to drive out demons. ¹⁶ So Jesus appointed the Twelve.

OBEY IT
If you haven't noticed by now, serving people can be exhausting, even frustrating. In times when you want to give up, remember three important things:
1. The *Person* who calls you is important! Jesus called his disciples two thousand years ago, and he calls his disciples still. A sense of call is especially important during difficult times, because sometimes *all* you have is your call.
2. The *Purpose* why He called you is important. Recognize **why** He called you. Notice the three things that the disciples were able to do, after their call. Cast out demons. Preach. Heal. Sometimes the real purpose why Jesus called us gets lost. He called us to be with Him! We are to *be*, before we *do*.
3. The *Personality* of those he called with you is important. A close look at the personality of the disciples reveals anything else but uniformity. They were different, and that was a good thing. Different backgrounds. Different social status. Different politics. Different jobs. What message was Jesus trying to send us through the picking of the disciples? A simple one. If Jesus was able to transform and use them, he can do the same with me. Service for others was their common denominator.

SHARE IT
1. Be a courteous driver.
2. Hold the elevator.
3. Visit a lemonade stand or a corner food vendor and buy something.

My Prayer Today:
Lord, help me remember that I am a human being, not a human doing. That I must be with you, before I can work for you. Amen.

My Thoughts _____

_____

PART I DAY 20 — VISION

SEE IT
1 Samuel 14:1 One day Jonathan said to his armor bearer, "Come on, let's go over to where the Philistines have their outpost." But Jonathan **did not tell** his father what he was doing.

OBEY IT
Suppose for a moment, that you are Jonathan. If you had a plan to attack the enemy, wouldn't the logical choice for sharing that valuable bellic information be the king, who was also your father? Yet, Jonathan chose not to share his plan. Be careful who you share your vision with. Why careful?

1. **Some will get upset.** They don't like the fact that it wasn't their idea.
2. **Some will oppose it.** They don't like the fact that it wasn't them who was chosen.
3. **Some will laugh at it.** They see silliness where you see success.
4. **Some will question it.** They say "You sure?", not "how can I help you?"

Here is some practical advice. Once you are convinced that God has in fact given you a vision, when someone comes to give you the all the reasons why it won't work, you can take criticism in stride. Don't discount criticism altogether, it can be the sandpaper that can polish the work of art God and you are building. At the same time, don't let criticism stop progress. Whatever God blesses the devil attacks. While you don't want to be reckless and irresponsible with your decisions going forward, you do want to step out in faith. Most great inventions, as well as almost every great accomplishment had two things in common:

1. Was conceived by a visionary.
2. Was opposed or dismissed by many.

So, march ahead and serve your community in Jesus name.

SHARE IT
1. Visit a senior center or nursing home.
2. Say "thank you" for the otherwise routine, mundane.
3. Pick up trash.

My Prayer Today:
Father, I have a passion to serve my community but sometimes I run into opposition from people inside and outside of my church. Help me to see what you see and continue. Amen.

My Thoughts _____

_____

GIVING

PART I
DAY 21

SEE IT
Proverbs 19:17 If you help the **poor**, you are lending to the Lord— and he will repay you!

OBEY IT
Grace is free, but ministry takes resources. If God has blessed you, he did so that you can be a blessing to others. He gave you money for 3 reasons:

1. It should be saved. Financial experts say that at least five percent of what we earn should be saved every time we're paid. When we save, we do three things:
   a. We're preparing for the unexpected.
   b. We're making sure our children will have a better chance for success.
   c. We're obeying what the Bible commands.

2. It should be shared. When we give, we benefit others and advance the kingdom of God on Earth. A philanthropist once said, "I give my money with a shovel to God, and He does the same. But the interesting thing is that His shovel is a lot bigger than mine." When we give first to God, we are declaring spiritually that we are givers first and consumers second.

3. It should be enjoyed. The following biblical passage clearly establishes this principle: "Moreover, when God gives any man wealth and possessions, and enables him to *enjoy* them, to accept his lot and be *happy* in his work—this is a gift of God. (Ecclesiastes 5:19, emphasis supplied). We must avoid extremes. We should not consume addictively but should spend wisely, and from time to time do some fun things and participate in activities we can enjoy, especially if we have families. How will you use the resources God has given you to bless others this week?

SHARE IT
1. Pay the toll for the person behind you.
2. Tape a nice saying or thought to a bus window.
3. Donate one of your favorite possessions. Or 10% of your clothing.

My Prayer Today:
Father, help me realize how blessed I am. Thanks for allowing me to bless someone today that is less fortunate than myself. Amen.

My Thoughts _____

_____

PART I
DAY 22

SERVING

SEE IT
Mathew 23:5 "Everything they do is done for men to see: They make their phylacteries wide, and the tassels on their garments long,"

OBEY IT
Every act has its motivation. God not only sees the acts, He knows the intentions of the heart. Have you ever asked yourself, "Why do I serve?" These are some of the common motivators for serving:

- Habit: That's what you were taught; you got used to serving.
- Obligation: If you don't serve, you can't take part, so you serve.
- Fear: If you stop serving, you worry something bad might happen to you.
- Peer Pressure: Everyone in your family and church serves, so you also serve.
- You Were Asked: Someone asked you to serve, so you serve.
- Self-interest: You want more blessings. You've heard that if you serve, you will get it.
- Influence: When you serve in significant ways, your opinion seems to count more.
- Legalism: You believe that the act of serving wins you salvation, or at least it helps.
- Competition: You want your church, group, or family to serve more than _____.

Why do you serve? What is the real reason? Let's serve simply:

- Because God served us first. Let's serve because of what God did.
- Because we want God to know that we recognize His sovereignty and power over our lives.
- Because we love God and can't keep from serving. Not serving is no longer an option.

SHARE IT
1. Let someone get ahead of you in line.
2. Listen intently.
3. Prepare a nutritious sack lunch for a homeless person.

My Prayer Today:
Jesus, I want to serve you and your people for the right reasons. Help me do that. Amen.

My Thoughts

BEYOND

**PART I
DAY 23**

SEE IT
2 Corinthians 8:2-3 "Out of the most severe trial, their overflowing joy and their extreme poverty welled up in rich generosity. For I testify that they gave as much as they were able, and even **beyond** their ability,"

OBEY IT
When I talk to married couples, I ask them, "What is one of the most dangerous enemies of a home?" The response may seem strange, but it's true. It's the **routine** filled life. Today being the same as yesterday, which was the same as the day before. Different date in the calendar but it's the same thing. Monotony kills love, withers away passion, and dampens relationships. How does this apply to service? I have three challenges for you:

1. Leave your comfort zone. Give more than you think you can. Give until it hurts. Agree with God that you will pay for or participate in some service project in your local church, support an evangelistic endeavor in the community, or help a person in need. Then do it, once and for all, and put God to the test. Go beyond your ability.

2. If you want to have what you've never had before, give what you've never given before. In other words, if you keep on giving as you've always done before, you'll keep on having what you've always had before. Isn't it time to rise to the next level? Go beyond your comfort level.

3. Don't wait for conditions to be right, serve today. If you wait for all conditions to be just right, you probably will never serve. We don't want to be reckless. We also don't want to miss what God is about to do. Ask God to open doors and then walk through them. Serve in something that stretches you. Go beyond your possibilities.

SHARE IT
1. Let things go. Laugh heartily at yourself.
2. Share your last bit.
3. Stop everything to help someone else.

My Prayer Today:
Lord, I give you permission to stretch me, challenge me and push me. Help me go "beyond". Amen.

My Thoughts _____

_____

**PART I
DAY 24**

BLESSING

SEE IT
Genesis 12:2 "I will make you into a great nation and I will bless you; I will make your name great, and you will be a blessing,"

OBEY IT
How will you complete this text?: "You will be made rich in every way so _____," 2 Corinthians 9:11. Some answer, so…

- I can live well.
- I can pay my bills.
- I can provide for my family.
- I can pay off my house.
- I can have economic security.

If God, in his infinite mercy, tomorrow should send you a check for one million, what would you do with it? How would you impact the world? How would you help your community? I encourage you to outline a plan where you help your community, beginning today. Think big and dream beyond what you see at the moment. Prepare to put into practice that which you want to accomplish when your opportunity comes, but start doing something small today. This 40 day devotional is a way for you to keep these concepts fresh in your mind and fulfill the real purpose for which God blesses us. Here is that text: "You will be made rich in every way so that you can be *generous* on every occasion, and through us your generosity will result in thanksgiving to God," 2 Corinthians 9:11 (emphasis supplied).

SHARE IT
1. Plant a tree.
2. Send a teacher flowers or an appreciation letter.
3. Write a thank you letter to your parents.

My Prayer Today:
Lord, help me be generous. Consistently. Amen.

My Thoughts _____

_____

SEASON OF SERVICE

GRACE

PART I
DAY 25

SEE IT
2 Corinthians 8:7-9 "But since you excel in everything—in faith, in speech, in knowledge, in complete earnestness and in the love we have kindled in you—see that you also excel in this grace of giving. I am not commanding you, but I want to test the sincerity of your love by comparing it with the earnestness of others. For you know the grace of our Lord Jesus Christ, that though he was rich, yet for your sake he became poor, so that you through his poverty might become rich,"

OBEY IT
People who have experienced God's grace understand three things:
1. They understand the connection between grace and generosity. Before anything else, we must realize that such a connection does exist. Many Christians do not understand this concept. A saved person is a generous person. If I'm drowning and someone saves me, how do I respond to that gesture? If I'm dying of heart failure and someone donates his or her heart to save my life, how do I react? The clear answer is "with generosity".
2. They understand that generosity is evidence of their salvation. Generosity doesn't buy our salvation; it's evidence of our salvation. The more clearly we visualize the sacrifice of Jesus, the wider we will open our hands to help others. As Jesus opened His hands on the cross and blessed the whole world in giving up His life, we, His followers, open our hands and bless our world, as we give with selfless generosity.
3. They understand the implication of being generous. Today's text tells us that when Jesus gave, our situation improved. This is the implication of giving. Other people do better. Other people progress. Other people change. Other people are saved. What better reward than to change the life of another person?

SHARE IT
1. Give someone a fruit basket.
2. Leave a good book in a public place with a note.
3. Donate books to your local library.

My Prayer Today:
Lord, thank you for saving me. I could never repay it, but I will extend to others the same grace you extended to me. Amen.

My Thoughts _____

_____

**PART I
DAY 26**

TODAY

SEE IT
Psalms 39:4-7   "Show me, LORD, my life's end and the number of my days; let me know how fleeting my life is. You have made my days a mere handbreadth; the span of my years is as nothing before you. Everyone is but a breath, even those who seem secure. Surely everyone goes around like a mere phantom; in vain they rush about, heaping up wealth without knowing whose it will finally be. But now, Lord, what do I look for? My hope is in you," Psalm 39:4-7.

OBEY IT
Three dangers of leaving until tomorrow what you can do today:
1. Today, you are the answer to someone's prayer. One of the acts of God, through His Spirit, consists of connecting the needs of His children with those who can fill those needs. If God impresses your heart to give or do something now is the time. Postponing our generosity is to disobey. The moment you receive the conviction to give or do and you say, "Later," you're saying, "I decide."
2. You are alive today, but you know nothing about your tomorrow. If you understand that to serve is a privilege, you would be depriving yourself of that benefit by postponing your service. Notice in today's text all the words that speak about the shortness of life: "Fleeting." "As nothing." "But a breath." "A mere phantom." The psalmist described what many ignore: Tomorrow is not guaranteed; you can only work and serve today.
3. You can decide what you do today; tomorrow another will do it for you. While we are alive, we can decide how, where, how much, and to whom our donations and actions will flow. After we die, though we may leave a will, the control is left in other hands which do not always reflect our same interests. Because you're alive today, do good to others today.

SHARE IT
1. Send anonymous flowers to your office receptionist or someone who works near you.
2. Buy an extra umbrella for a rainy day.
3. Give your waiter or waitress a larger than usual tip.

My Prayer Today:
Lord, I recognize that tomorrow is not guaranteed. Can you help me do something today? Amen.

My Thoughts _____

_____

TIMELY

SEE IT
Ecclesiastes 3:12 "There is a **time** for everything, and a season for every activity under heaven. I know that there is nothing better for men than to be happy and **do good** while they live"

OBEY IT
There are three ways to manage your time in such a way that you can serve others.
1. Slow down. In a recent study, 50 percent surveyed said they "want to slow down, but don't know how." How do you slow down? One way is to realize that you will never finish everything you have to do. Never! So slow down today, notice the needs of people around you. How can we practice this? When will you slow down?
2. Seek God. As you slow down, make sure you include intentional times of prayer and reading of the Word, as well as times for fasting. Ask God to reveal to you hurting people that surround you, and when He does, minister to them. What's the best time of day for you to connect with God?
3. Set goals. Author Brian Tracy says that for every minute you spend planning the day before, you save 10 minutes the next day. How clear are your goals? What specific goals do you have for serving others this year? This week? This decade?

SHARE IT
1. Prepare a "to-go" breakfast for the morning mailman.
2. Mail a friend some cupcakes.
3. Tape an anonymous clean funny joke to your boss' monitor.

My Prayer Today:
Lord, help me slow down and notice other's needs. Help me manage my time in such a way that I am able to minister to those around me. Amen.

My Thoughts _____

_____

PART I — DAY 28

POOR

SEE IT
Proverbs 19:17 "However, there need be no poor people among you, for in the land the LORD your God is giving you to possess as your inheritance, he will richly bless you," Deuteronomy 15:4. "Whoever is kind to the poor lends to the LORD, and he will reward them for what they have done,"

OBEY IT
Today we can learn these two lessons:
1. Though you cannot help all the poor, you can begin by helping one. This story encapsulates what I mean: "One morning as I walked along the seashore, I saw a young man who would bend down, then straighten up, over and over again. As I drew closer, I could see he wasn't dancing, but was searching among the debris that the night tide had brought in. He would bend down, pick up a starfish, and throw it back into the sea. I asked him what he was doing. "The tide brought these creatures up, onto the beach, and now they can't get back alone," the young man replied. "When the sun comes up, they'll die, unless they are returned to the ocean." I looked out over the vast expanse of the beach. An incalculable number of starfish covered the sand. "But there are more starfish on this beach than you can possible save before daybreak. Surely you don't expect to make a difference here," I replied. The young man paused, as if meditating on what I had said, then he bent down again, picked up a starfish, and threw it as far out into the water as he could. Then he said: "I just made a difference for that one."
2. Christians need to focus on helping the poor. Rob Graham, son of Billy Graham, said, "If you do not know the poor, or are not known by the poor, you have a crisis at the center of your Christianity. To know and to be known by the poor is essential."

SHARE IT
1. Volunteer at a soup kitchen.
2. Build a home with Habitat for Humanity.
3. Give a donation to ADRA or Compassion International.

My Prayer Today:
Lord, there are poor people in my community that need you and need me. Help me bring your love to their lives today. Amen.

My Thoughts _____

_____

SEASON OF SERVICE

LIGHT

**PART I
DAY 29**

SEE IT
Matthew 5:16 "Let your light so shine before men, that they may see your good works and glorify your Father in heaven."

OBEY IT
There are four ways our good works glorify our Father as our text says.
1. **Our good works can be like a beacon light at an airport that gives direction to planes wanting to land safely.** Our words, actions and attitude can reveal our Father in heaven and glorify Him.
2. **Our good works can be like a light illuminating this dark world.** Our words, actions and attitude can light this dark world and show what is right and wrong, thus glorifying our Father.
3. **Our good works can be like the safety lights installed in areas of criminal activity.** Our generosity can reveal greed, our love can reveal hate and prejudices , our kindness can reveal rudeness, our faith in God can reveal disparity and lack of trust, our assurance in salvation reveals the fear of the future, our hope reveals hopelessness, our faith in the living Jesus reveals the dead hope of those whose leaders are dead and we could go on and on as we live our faith today to glorify our Father and make our world safer and better place.
4. **Our good works reveals Jesus the Light of this world.** A Christian is Christ like. By our words, actions and attitude we reveal Jesus and glorify our Father.

SHARE IT
1. Visit an animal shelter.
2. Visit an orphanage or shelter with some goodies.
3. Invite a neighbor over for dinner with your family.

My Prayer Today: For people looking for light.
1. That God will use me to share the light in practical tangible ways.
2. That people that want the light will find the light through my love.

My Thoughts _____

_____

PART I — DAY 30

⟩ OBEDIENCE ⟨

SEE IT
Psalm 143:10 "Teach me to do Your will, for You are my God; may Your good Spirit lead me on level ground."

OBEY IT
Now, God has asked us to serve our community. Are we willing to obey Him? There are three reasons why obedience is important:

1. Obedience is for our protection. "Get down on the ground!" was the missionary's command to his son. They had been in Africa for just a few months and had gone for a walk away from the village. The son walked towards a tree to seek some shelter from the heat. The father saw a Black Mamba ready to strike his son. The father knew that its bite was 100 percent lethal. He called out to his son, "Get down on the ground." The son had no idea why his father asked him to do so, but because he loved and respected his father, he promptly obeyed. It was that obedience that saved the young man's life. The same way, obedience to God as we serve others protects us from one of our greatest enemies: greed and self.

2. Obedience is also for our *progression*. What God desires for us is for our good. When He asks us to obey, it is to help us grow and progress to a more enhanced life. When we obey Him and serve others, we grow. Simple, yet true.

3. Most importantly, our obedience is proof of our love for God. "Whoever has My commandments and keeps them is the one who loves Me." John 14:21. When we don't obey, we are putting ourselves and our desires above our love for God. The paradox of this reality is that the more we love God and put Him before our desires, the more blessed our lives will be. The more we seek for ourselves, the less we will have. The proof is in the service.

SHARE IT
1. Leave a collection of positive news clippings in a waiting room.
2. Turn off a leaky faucet, flush a toilet, clean a sink.
3. Babysit for a single parent or a young couple so that they can have a night out.

My Prayer Today:
Lord, help me be obedient to your will. I want to serve those around me today. Help me do that. Amen.

My Thoughts _____
_____

EXPECT

PART I
DAY 31

SEE IT
Psalm 5:2-3 NLT "Listen to my cry for help, my King and my God, for I will never pray to anyone but you. Listen to my voice in the morning, Lord. Each morning I bring my request to you and wait expectantly."

OBEY IT
What can we learn from these verses today?
1. We are in desperate need of help and there is only One who can help. God, our Creator and King is waiting for us to bring our problems to Him. When you see the state of our communities and our world, we may despair. But when we look up, we can have hope.
2. We need daily consistent prayer.
Not only is it important to come to God in prayer, we also need to make it a daily matter. As we spend time each day with God we come to realize how much He really loves us and wants to help us with the difficulties we face in life. We learn to trust Him as our closest friend and we look forward to and cherish each moment we can spend with Him. Prayer is a great way to find out from God who we can help today.
3. We should expect that God will answer our earnest petitions.
God is sympathetic toward our trials and concerns and He is able to help us to deal with and give solutions to our problems, because He is a God of power. Without wavering we should believe He will answer our prayers and fulfill our requests as long as we are in His will and are willing to obey Him. We are to expect good things from God. The Christian life is an expectant life. Our greatest expectation is the soon second coming of Christ when the culmination of all our expectations will be realized. In this hope, we can go and serve others.

SHARE IT
1. Read to a child.
2. Rake someone's yard.
3. Recycle.

My Prayer Today: I pray that people realize that there is a God in Heaven who answers prayer. I Pray that others will see how we as Christians live in joyful expectation. I Pray that others will come to know God as a loving Savior and friend who wants to answer their requests when they pray. Amen.

My Thoughts _____

_____

PART I DAY 32

COACH

SEE IT
Romans 4:17 "(as it is written, "I have made you a father of many nations") in the presence of Him who believed-God, who gives life to the dead and calls those 'things which do not exist as though they did:"

OBEY IT
We can learn three lessons from today's text:
1. God is the One with the game plan. Today's text begins with "as it is written." Our heavenly Father knows about our life and the challenges and perplexities we face. As His children it's important to remember that there is nothing we will encounter that will take Him by surprise. This is especially important when serving others. Instead of asking God to bless the plans we come up with, let's ask Him what His plan is and join him.
2. God is the One who call the plays. So often we feel as if our lives are just a scrambled up mess. We face uncertainty on every front. Our faith is tested by the circumstances we encounter. That was certainly the case for Abraham. Who could have imagined him becoming the father of us all with his barren wife and his old worn out body? Yet God's promise and His Word is sure. He knows the end from the beginning and His ultimate goal is for us to be victorious in this life and to have an eternal place with Him.
3. God is the One who knows His team. He has chosen us of all people to represent His cause on this planet. Though we are sinners, He calls us saints. Though we are weak, through faith in Him, we become strong. Everything He promised to us, He will deliver. Psalm 56:9 says, "When I cry out to you, Then my enemies will turn back; This I know because God is for me." That is what a great coach is noted for...being "for me" and that makes all the difference. He sees possibilities where I can only see struggles. He sees victories where I can only see failures. He sees gains where I can only see losses. So, go forth and serve in confidence. We win!

SHARE IT
1. Wave and smile to the person in the car next to you at a street intersection.
2. Be bold in your appreciation of life around you. Let people know that you appreciate them.
3. Create or buy a piece of art and gift it to someone

My Prayer for Today:
Lord, that I would know the assurance of being on God's team. Please put me in a position to share the gospel today. Especially with those that need your grace the most. Amen.
My Thoughts

CREATE

PART I
DAY 33

SEE IT
Revelation 21:5 Then He who sat on the throne said, "Behold, I make all things new." And He said to me, "Write, for these words are true and faithful." (NKJV)

OBEY IT
We can learn three lessons from today's text.
1. The One who speaks is seated on the throne. The throne is a position of authority which means that anyone who speaks *from* that position *possess* authority. The words that follow aren't merely a good idea or a possibility. Moreover, God sits on the throne—his words will become actions because he has the power and right to make it so. Believe in God's authority.
2. God makes all things new. As I reflect on the death of a friend's father and on another friend whose house sustained severe fire damage, I'm reminded that life is unpredictable and that "new" is what we desperately need. God will create again. Everything will get a new start. And this is not only a future plan but also a present reality. God continually makes things new. This is the Gospel. This is love. Believe in God as Creator.
3. God doesn't lie. Sometimes it's easy to believe that since there are many corrupt leaders out there, sitting in seats of authority but not doing the good they promised, there's no guarantee that God will actually do what he said. But God doesn't lie. As confusing as life can be, God has always been faithful. No, he doesn't always provide answers that we think make sense—that is true. Yet God has proven to be steadfast in the midst of our confusion—he still wants to save us, which is why he gives us one opportunity after another to embrace his love. Believe in God's faithfulness. Share your stories of God's creative power with others. Let them know of the new things God has done in your life. This will strengthen someone else's walk and will serve as a wonderful reminder to you during those moments when your faith is weak.

SHARE IT
1. Put up anonymous, encouraging post-it notes for strangers to find.
2. Donate blood.
3. Cook dinner for a busy parent.

My Prayer Today: For those who are anxious for God to create something new
I pray today that God will send reminders of his faithfulness and that we will trust God's plans and creative power to bring renewal and revival to our churches and communities. Amen.

My Thoughts _____

PART I — DAY 34

WORDS

SEE IT
Mathew 8:5 When Jesus returned to Capernaum, a Roman officer came and pleaded with him, [6] "Lord, my young servant lies in bed, paralyzed and in terrible pain." [7] Jesus said, "I will come and heal him." [8] But the officer said, "Lord, I am not worthy to have you come into my home. Just say the word from where you are, and my servant will be healed.

OBEY IT
There are three principles we can learn today:
1. The words of Jesus have the same power as His presence. We do not have the physical presence of Jesus among us now, but we have His Word. When we claim the promises of Jesus in our lives, we see the same power working in us that we would have if Jesus were physically present.
2. Our faith is demonstrated by the way we speak. As we saw the faith of the centurion by the way he talked, other people are going to see our faith by how we express ourselves. In this season of service, people will be watching us. What will they hear? The people in our communities are looking for people that speak the truth, with love. Do you?
3. Words without power are not effective. One of the texts today taught us that words must be accompanied by power. That means not just talking. While words reveal our faith, actions confirm our faith. We are to put our faith into action! Who do you know that talks a lot but does little? How annoying is that! Let the words of our mouths be accompanied with actions from our hands.

SHARE IT
1. Give a little one a lollipop.
2. Make time.
3. Speak gently.

My Prayer Today:
Lord Jesus, let the words that I speak to other people reflect your work in my life. Amen.

My Thoughts _____
_____

UNITY

**PART I
DAY 35**

SEE IT
1 Samuel 14:7 "Do what you think is best," the armor bearer replied. "I'm with you completely, whatever you decide."
In this Biblical story, Jonathan understood that while it's easier to do something alone, it's more effective when we involve others. There is a small word, with big power, and that word is *and*. It's one thing to say, it's me. Another thing to say, it's me *and* my church. What we sometimes fail to understand in this polarized society, is that we need each other. Unity multiplies impact.

OBEY IT
God created us for community. God is emphatic about giving the vision to the leader first, but not exclusively. A right vision, shared with the right people, at the right time, for the right reason, will accomplish more, in less time. Here are some of the people you'll need:
1. Mentors. These are wise people you can *listen* to. They have experience and can help you find ways better serve your community.
2. Friends. These are caring people you can *lean* on. They might not have all the answers, but knowing that they are there for you makes a difference. These are people that will go alongside you to reach your community.
3. Students. These people who can *learn* from you. Every experience you have had is a lesson that can be shared to encourage, inspire, or warn others. They will learn from you what to do and not to do, to reach the community.
In order to finish the work God has entrusted to us we need everybody. Traditional *and* contemporary, men *and* women, youth *and* adults, 1st *and* 2nd generation, accredited colleges and self-supporting ministries. lay members *and* paid denominational employees. We are one church. When we attack each other it creates confusion in our youth, discouragement in our members, and delay in our progress. If we are going to impact, we must do so as one.

SHARE IT
1. Intentionally serve and help someone who does not agree with you on an issue.
2. Offer someone an unexpected tip.
3. Take a bottle of water and offer it to a co-worker.

My Prayer Today:
Jesus, help me play well with others. Amen.

My Thoughts _____

_____

PART I — DAY 36

GUESTS

SEE IT
Acts 15:19 "And so my judgment is that we **should not** make it difficult for the Gentiles who are turning to God.

OBEY IT
Part of the Season of Service is paying special attention to guests that come into our churches. What do you do when they arrive? Pay attention to what guests experience in these areas:

1. What they hear. Do you keep the service positive? Is the Sabbath school director happy about the ones that are there, or is complaining about the ones that aren't? Are you prone to speaking adventese or can guests clearly understand? When offering time comes, does it paint a picture of vision and progress or is it a list of complaints about bills, past dues and lack of commitment from members? People give, are attracted to, and inspired by a positive vision, not a litany of complaints.

2. What they see. Clear signage is important. You know where bathrooms, children's classrooms, the sanctuary and the fellowship hall are. Do they? No! Another thing they see is clutter. The longer you are in a church the less you see the broken window held with duct tape, the ceiling that has water spots, the year old bulletins in the classrooms, the boxes, hymnals out of place, broken things in the parking lot and rusty chairs. The message that sends is this: We don't care about our church. Neither should you. Please don't come here. Were good.

3. What they smell. Churches with musty smells, that reek of unattractive odors, send the message: today's service is to be endured, not enjoyed. Andy Stanley in his book Deep & Wide, says it best: "the physical environment does more than leave an impression; it sends a message." What changes can you make? Who can be a set of fresh eyes you could invite to take a look at your church and point out some areas of growth?

SHARE IT
1. Prepare a gift bag for the visitors that will come to church this weekend.
2. Take some soup or hot chocolate to a homeless person
3. Buy a positive, uplifting, movie and give it to a young person in your neighborhood.

My Prayer Today:
Heavenly Father, help me make the experience of the guests in my church memorable. Help me to neither ignore or overwhelm them. Amen.

My Thoughts _____

_____

LOVE

PART I — DAY 37

SEE IT
Luke 19:41 But as he came closer to Jerusalem and saw the city ahead, he began to *weep*".
Luke 13:34 'O *Jerusalem, Jerusalem*, the city that kills the prophets and stones God's messengers! How often I have wanted to gather your children together as a hen protects her chicks beneath her wings, but you wouldn't let me' ".

OBEY IT
We can learn three lessons from today's text.
1. Sinful lifestyle doesn't deter a demonstration of love. Jerusalem had a history of being a "city that kills the prophets and stones God's messengers" and that refused to be corrected ("you wouldn't let me"). Yet, Jesus loved it, ministered to it, preached in it, and sought to transform it anyway!
2. Instead of leaving, love. When Jesus saw the need, He went toward and not away from Jerusalem. He knew very well that the treatment He would receive there would not be pleasant, but His heart longed to save the people of the city.
3. Love is more than a feeling *for* the city, it is action *in* the city. Jesus cried for the city and had compassion for the people living there. That was wonderful, but not enough. He took those feelings and put them into action as He healed, preached, and helped. The purpose of these lessons is to spur you and your congregation to action.

SHARE IT
1. Stamps in Front of the Post Office. One church holds a major stamp outreach on April 15th for late tax-filers. Volunteers stand by the mail drop-off boxes with a card table filled with food and stamps.
2. Gatorade at Biking Trails. Some health-conscious folks like runners, bikers, and other people don't drink soda at all. Set up at along a bike trail, athletic field, or hiking trail and offer Gatorade or bottled water to exercisers.
3. Pay Library Fines. Leave $20.00 at the front desk in the local library, and instruct the clerk to use it for the next person who has fines.

My Prayer Today:
Lord, help me love my city, not leave it. Help me do all that can to show them. Amen.

My Thoughts _____

_____

**PART I
DAY 38**

◆ **IMPACT** ◆

SEE IT
Mark 10:45 "For even the Son of Man did not come to be *served*, but to *serve*, and to give his life as a ransom for many".

OBEY IT
Three important principles we can learn from this lesson are:
1. Service broadens your impact. When we serve, we impact three groups of people in a positive way—the one who serves, the ones you serve, and the ones you serve with. This is especially important for the younger generation, who love to see the church engaging the community in practical ways.
2. Service honors God, blesses people, and changes perceptions. A leading proponent of servant evangelism puts it this way: "Servant evangelism softens the hearts of persons who are not yet Christians—people who often think the church exists only for itself or that it only wants people's time and money. By doing a 'low-risk' activity that shows 'high grace,' those resistant to the faith may (now or in the future) become more open to the saving message of Jesus Christ."
3. Service is more than an event. It is not something we do once in a while to placate the conscience, appease the leadership, or satisfy a requirement. In order to make this a priority in our churches, we must do four things: Schedule it. Fund it. Model it. Speak about it.

SHARE IT
1. Bait at Local Fishing Spots: Those who fish with live bait need worms, grubs, goldfish, minnows, or whatever. Purchase these critters in large quantities from a bait shop, go
to the local fishing hot-spot and give them away.
2. Pay Laundromat Washer and Dryer: Bring a roll or two of quarters and dimes. As patrons enter, ask them if they'd like hot or cold wash. You can also provide detergent. Note: This works best for women—it's a bit odd for men to reach out to women in this setting.
3. Hand Cleaning Towelettes: Pretty much everything in downtown shopping areas is a bit dirty, but there's really no place to wash up. Give them this.

My Prayer Today:
Lord, help me understand how service can impact our world for you. Amen.

My Thoughts _____

_____

SEASON OF SERVICE

◆ INVITATION ◆

**PART I
DAY 39**

SEE IT
Matthew 25:35 "For I was hungry and you gave me something to eat, I was thirsty and you gave me something to drink, I was a stranger and you *invited* me in".

OBEY IT
Eventually God will open doors to invite people to church. When that happens, remember:
1. **Inviting is more effective when it's done in the context of relationships.** We get invited all the time through emails, flyers, or TV advertising with various degrees of success. Nothing beats an invitation from a friend. I invite you to maximize the relationships you already have. Remember to invite **F.R.A.N.C**. That stands for friends, relatives, associates, neighbors, coworkers.
2. **Inviting is more effective when you know "why."** The invitation you are about to give can in fact bring the following three benefits: (1) it can change a life; (2) it can transform a family's history; (3) it can advance God's kingdom. The disciples knew why. Our pioneers knew why. Do you know why?

SHARE IT
1. Trash Pick-up for Students near Campuses: Consider visiting on Sunday afternoons around two, so you'll catch everybody waking up from their Saturday nights.
2. Post Cards and Stamps: College students do actually write home on occasion. Provide postcards complete with postage with a sticker that reads, "It's good to write your mom!" Include your connection card.
3. Photocopying: Purchase photocopying coupons at a reduced rate at a local copy center near the college campus. The price shouldn't be more than about five cents per copy. Give these punch cards out on campus. Place church logo and phone number on the card.

My Prayer Today:
Jesus, help me bold enough to invite people, loving enough to do it, and discerning enough to know when to do it. Amen.

My Thoughts _____

_____

PART I — DAY 40

CHANGE

SEE IT
Jonah 1:1 The LORD gave this message to Jonah son of Amittai: ² "Get up and go to the great city of Nineveh. Announce my judgment against it because I have seen how wicked its people are."³ But Jonah got up and went in the opposite direction to get away from the LORD. He went down to the port of Joppa, where he found a ship leaving for Tarshish. He bought a ticket and went on board, hoping to escape from the LORD by sailing to Tarshish.

OBEY IT
Jonah was an interesting character. He was doing his thing, in a small town. Solid guy. Faithful. Constant. Then God (as he usually does) messed up his plans. He called him to change 3 things:

1. Change in location. Jonah was a good small parish pastor. He had family in town. He was well liked. He knew the people and the people knew him. Then God "ruins" his best laid plans. He told him to go where no one knew, liked, respected or was related to him, at great peril to his life. What if God did that to you? Would you go?

2. Change in his ministry objective. God told Jonah to change his target. He went from a small town prophet to a mission to the big city. Much like Jonah's contemporaries, we have also abandoned the cities. Instead of leaving the city, we must be loving the city. God gave him two reasons to go: a. It is a large city. (potential for great impact) b. It is wicked. (great need for God) That call hasn't changed. Large cities are not to be left alone. We must give the last warning.

3. Change in strategy. God told Jonah to "get up and go". That was strange. The people of Israel didn't "go". Others came. Others were invited in. You come to us, not us to you, was the modus operandi. God calls him to a paradigm shift. To a different strategy. He wanted Jonah to understand that our job is not only to bring people to church, but to take church to the people.

SHARE IT
1. Send a nice card to a family member, just because.
2. Don't lose any opportunity to say: i love you.
3. Leave a funny or kind note in an unexpected place.

My Prayer Today:
Lord, restore in me the passion to love the city where I live. To resolve to love them, not leave them. Amen.

◆ FINAL THOUGHTS ◆

**PART I
DAY 40**

Final Thoughts:
In the story of Jonah, we find a great deal of symbolism. Jonah was asked to go to Nineveh. Have any of us been given a mission field? Nineveh is a symbol then for our mission field. Our mission field may be our family, our community, our workplace, the marketplace, or all of the above. The important thing to note here is that it is God who chooses our mission field, not us. If we do the choosing, we will wind up in Tarshish every time. Tarshish, of course, is the place, activity, lifestyle that we choose. The problem with us doing the choosing is that we, of ourselves, have no spiritual nature. So, we *always* choose wrong. That's why we need God's Holy Spirit in our lives. It's also why God's promise to send His Holy Spirit, every time we ask, is unconditional.

We may be sure that God will choose a mission field that is within our "Potential Sphere of Influence". However, it may not be the one that we are the most comfortable with. Faith will play an active part in our acceptance of God's choice. We may be equally certain that He will take into account the unique combination of talents that He has blessed us with.

You may be asking how you can know what God's choice is. How did Jonah know? He heard God's voice…didn't he? Do you realize that God, the Holy Spirit, is constantly "Talking" to you as He seeks to guide you into the path that He has chosen for your life? Granted, in all likelihood, it's not audible; but His spiritual voice is always available to you.

As you tune in on a daily basis to that voice and tune out the clamor of the world, in prayer and Bible study, it will become more and more discernible to you. As a matter of fact it would not be inappropriate to point out that if you don't hear that voice, you're not ready for a mission field.

Because he went to the mission field of God's choosing under duress, we should understand that Jonah is a type of those Christians who seek to do the work of the church without a changed heart. There are many Christians who outwardly conform to the requirements of their faith by force of will alone. They seek to follow God in their own strength. They also tend to be judgmental of less successful church members.

Was Jonah successful? Yes he was very successful!!! After three days of preaching every person from the King to the pauper was converted. Did you ever wonder why Jonah preached for forty days when everyone repented after three days? There was still one man in Nineveh that was unconverted. It was Jonah!!!

May God help us to be obedient to his call, to serve others and grow ourselves into the people he would like.

APPENDIX 1

100+ COMMUNITY SERVANT EVANGELISM IDEAS FOR YOUR CHURCH

APPENDIX 1

Steve Sjogren puts it this way concerning servant evangelism: "Servant Evangelism (SE) connects people to people in a natural, easy, low risk, high grace way. Who doesn't like to be given a cold drink on a hot day? Especially by someone who is smiling, happy and having fun. SE wins the heart before it confronts the mind. A small act of kindness nudges a person closer to God, often in a profound way as it bypasses ones mental defenses.

The average Christ-follower is willing to hand a stranger a water bottle (low risk). The high grace is seen in the typical reaction. "Oh, thank you!" "This is so nice!" "I can't believe this is for free!" And, "Why are you doing this?" Kindness builds the bridge for the person to receive a touch of love from God. Add an invitation to church or other method of connection—even a simple card

with your church's name, phone number and times of services—and you've reached someone with the love of Christ! It's simple, practical, effective, inexpensive and fun! We get reports from pastors, lay leaders and ordinary Christ-followers all over the world who have discovered the power and impact of "showing God's love in practical ways," and again and again we've seen relationships with God born from these simple acts of kindness in Christ's

name. Here are some great ideas to get your church started in servant evangelism.

EASY, LOW-COST GIVEAWAYS

1. Hot Drink Giveaways
Use either Igloo containers or air pump thermoses. Offer options. On a cool day, you will have folks swarming for a cup of something hot. You will need three or four people to help give away the hot drink for each big canister. With each drink, we give out a connection card. Consider having paper cups with your church's name and logo printed.

2. Newspapers
Some convenience stores will allow you to purchase an entire stack of newspapers. Place a sign on the top of the stack that reads, "Free Newspapers – Courtesy of (Church Name)" and attach a connection card to each paper with removable adhesive.

3. Donut Giveaway during Morning Traffic Times
This giveaway is especially effective when performed by senior citizens—who can say no to a sweet grandma-type? These gals set up on a traffic island at a stoplight (make sure they're safe out there). When the light turns red, they step up to cars and ask, "Would you like chocolate, maple or glazed?" They then give them a connection card with the snack.

4. Gatorade Giveaways
"Hi, would you like something to quench your thirst?" This is our standard opening to bless folks with a small act of kindness on a hot day. And it works! We set up at grocery store entrances with large coolers filled with ice and drinks. Place a connection card under the opener. A

courtesy note: Sometimes a location will conflict with vendors selling what you are giving away. Some of the most irate critics we've run into have been vendors who conclude we are trying to put them out of business. The answer: Set up in a location away from vendors. In extreme cases, consider asking the vendor how much money he/she anticipates losing by our presence, then give them that amount in cash.

5. Bottled Water Giveaway
Many people prefer water to gatorade. Ice down bottles of water in large coolers for an alternative to a soft drink giveaway. Use the same connection cards.

6. LifeSavers
If you are looking for an affordable entry point for a large number of people, consider this one. We purchase the candy at a warehouse store for about five cents per roll. We attach a connection card and give out hundreds of these candies to passersby. Everyone will take a roll of these candies. Consider printing the message of the connection card onto mailing labels and sticking them over the top of the LifeSavers wrapper.

7. Lollipops / Blowpops
These are great giveaway items for parks, festivals, and college campuses. Purchase at a warehouse store for around six cents apiece, and fold a mailing label with connection information around the stick.

8. Popcorn
You can either make bags of popcorn before you arrive at your outreach site, or consider renting/purchasing your own carnival style popping machine and do it on the spot. You will draw more of a crowd with the machine on hand.

9. Sunglasses (cheap ones!)
Have you ever left home for a sporting event only to forget your sunglasses? Many sporting events attendees experience this every weekend. We have purchased large quantities of sunglasses for as little as a quarter a pair.

10. Ice Cream/Frozen Yogurt Coupons
Approach a local ice cream store and explain your desire to give away thousands of ice cream coupons. Chances are the owner/manager will be willing to give you a good deal on ice cream coupons. Attach a connection card to each coupon, and you'll have a project that will elicit a response from just about everyone in town.

SERVICES

11. Umbrella Escorts
Moms with kids and the elderly find it tough to make it from stores to their cars in the rain. We use huge golf umbrellas to help get them and their purchases to their cars with as little wetness as possible.

APPENDIX 1

12. Grocery Bag Loading Assistance
Moms with lots of kids hanging on them like koalas often need assistance getting their bags loaded into the car from the shopping cart. The elderly need the same sort of help. Volunteers on this project need to appear particularly safe and friendly; name tags or coordinating T-shirts identifying connection to your organization makes the servants look more "official." Note: On this project, almost everyone will try to give a tip, but as with all kindness projects, to receive money would taint what you are trying to communicate: "God's love in a practical package with no strings attached." This project may require permission from the store manager on the day of the event.

13. Bag-Packing at Self-Serve Grocers
Increasing numbers of grocery stores are cutting out services such as bag-packing. Place volunteers at these stores to pack bags for customers. Again, name tags or coordinating T-shirts or aprons helps the baggers look more official and identifies the connection with your organization.

14. Trash Pick-Up
There is lots of trash to pick up at festivals and sports events. Buy garbage bags, wear matching T-shirts and plastic gloves, and bring a sign to put up that says, "Kindness in Progress" while you pick up trash. People will notice.

15. Shoe Shines
Small investment + some elbow grease = big return. Set up in front of a grocery store on a Sunday, or perhaps in front of a barbershop. This is a great project to get talking with people; you have a captive audience while you serve!

16. Restroom Cleaning at Public Places
There's nothing like walking into a gas station, restaurant, or retail store and saying to the manager, "We'd like to clean your toilet for free!" Put a little cleaning kit together containing a toilet brush, air freshener, window cleaner, paper towels, toilet bowl cleaner, rubber gloves, and a doorstop.

AROUND TOWN

17. Business Blasts
Surprise employees of local businesses with a small gift, such as a basket of candy. Bring in one package to be shared by store employees and leave a connection card that reads something like, "We appreciate how you serve the community with your business, and we wanted to share God's love in a practical way." Make sure you only give items to employees, so they don't think you are "soliciting" their customers.

18. Drink Giveaway to Employees
What can you do when denied permission to give away drinks in front of a prime retail location? Offer to give them to the employees. As usual, place the connection card on top.

APPENDIX 1

19. Stamps in Front of the Post Office
Hold a major stamp outreach on April 15th for late tax-filers. Not only do they give out stamps, but they also offer something to eat—some stress recovery food. Volunteers stand by the mail drop-off boxes with a card table filled with food and stamps.

20. Gatorade at Biking Trails
Some health-conscious folks like runners, bikers, and other people don't drink soda at all. Set up at along a bike trail, athletic field, or hiking trail and offer Gatorade or bottled water to exercisers.

21. Pay Library Fines
Leave $20.00 at the front desk in the local library, and instruct the clerk to use it for the next person who has fines. Leave a connection card in an envelope for the person, so they can see why the fine was paid.

22. Surf Wax
Who says non-surfers can't relate to surfers? Buy the current popular brand of wax and hit the beach, dude! It's a definite door-, or rather board-, opener.

23. Pictionary in the Park
This was a popular game in the late 1980's similar to Charades. Set up in a local park and play the game using with a white board to draw hints. Complete strangers will start to join in, especially if your group is friendly and animated. When onlookers correctly guess the answer, allow them to play the next round. After 15-20 minutes, take a break, serve something to drink and talk to the visitors one-to-one.

24. Golf Balls
The average golfer loses three or four balls per outing, so give away imprinted golf balls on the local golf course. Imprinting your church's name and message on golf balls is surprisingly affordable, and if it's lost on the course, another golfer will pick it up later and get your message.

25. Golf Tees
Golfers can never get enough of these. Imprinted golf tees cost just a couple of cents apiece. Some golf courses will even give them away for you at their counter.

26. Golf Ball Cleaning
Sure, there are ball-cleaning machines spread throughout most golf courses, but most players don't take the time. With permission of the course, set up a simple clean up station and clean golf balls before golfers begin a round. Most golfers carry dozens of balls in their bag.

27. Cleaning Up at Food Courts
If you can get your foot in the door at your local mall, ask if you can do clean-up in the food court area. Along with a connection card, consider distributing handy-wipes with your logo imprinted on them.

28. Upsizing Food Orders in Fast Food Drive-Thru Lanes
Set-up near the drive-thru order station. As customers drive up, offer to

APPENDIX 1

pay the difference between their order and the bigger size—which is usually about 39 cents. Your offer will get the entire restaurant talking.

29. Free Bird Feeders and Refills to Convalescent Home Residents
Provide an acrylic bird feeder—the kind with suction cups that stick right to the window. Return occasionally to refill the bird feeder and check in on your new elderly friend. Note: Most outreaches to those in convalescent homes will touch their extended family, as well.

30. Bait at Local Fishing Spots
Those who fish with live bait need worms, grubs, goldfish, minnows, or whatever. Purchase these critters in large quantities from a bait shop, go to the local fishing hot-spot and give them away.

31. Pay Laundromat Washer and Dryer
Bring a roll or two of quarters and dimes. As patrons enter, ask them if they'd like hot or cold wash. You can also provide detergent. Note: This is a project that works best for women—it's a bit odd for men to reach out to women in this setting.

32. Instant Photos for Couples
A couple will hold on to a decent photo of themselves for years. Set up at a local carriage ride or other common spot for couples and take instant print photos of them. If you want to get fancy, offer a photo frame that is tailor-made for the size. Attach a sticker of your church's logo and phone number on the back.

33. Hand Cleaning Towelettes
Pretty much everything in downtown shopping areas is a bit dirty, but there's really no place to wash up. Give people these towelettes labeled with your organization's message.

34. Cart Token for Shopping Carts
Some grocery stores in urban areas require a token in order to get a shopping cart. Provide the tokens to shoppers as they enter.

35. Gasoline for Your Neighbor
How many people do you see buying less than a tank of gas when you fill 'er up? We see it happening all the time—they can't afford a full tank of gas at today's prices. Add $5.00 to their total and blow their minds. Of course, add in a connection card.

36. Food for Firefighters
Since 9/11, the general public has been made even more aware of the tremendous job that firefighters and police officers do day in and day out. Show them a little kindness by providing a delicious and healthy home cooked meal. Let them know in advance that you are coming. Firefighters are a great group to serve—they really appreciate it and talk a lot in the community.

NEIGHBORHOODS

37. Leaf Raking
"We came, we saw, we raked!" Several people in a small group can rake an entire neighborhood on a single Sunday morning/afternoon. Maybe

you don't like raking your own yard; but when you're with a group of friends serving in the name of Christ, a chore becomes a joy. Many yards take only fifteen to twenty minutes to polish off. Note: If possible, go to neighborhoods where the city vacuums leaves left on the curb (some do). If you bag them, make sure to remove the bags and dispose of them yourself instead of leaving them for the homeowners.

38. Lawn Mowing
Look for long grass, knock on the door, and go for it. Several mowers make this short work.

39. Grass Edging
If you don't have time to mow an entire lawn, edge the driveway and sidewalks. Most homeowners don't edge very often, so they are in need of it and are grateful.

40. Rain Gutter Cleaning
This is messy work but very appreciated by homeowners, especially in the fall. You will need some ladders, trash bags, and gloves.

41. Sidewalk Sweeping
In urban areas, this is a huge hit. Residents are sometimes required by neighborhood associations or city codes to sweep the area in front of their homes.

42. Screen Cleaning
Screens will have to be removed. Apply a bit of soapy water and use a soft brush. Hose them off and reinstall. Most homeowners never do this, though it is an easy way to improve the view.

43. Garbage Can Return from Street
This is a project you could do for an entire street each week. Usually garbage pick-up is done early in the morning—be the first one out. Return the cans to a place near each person's garage (but do it quietly!). Scotch tape a connection card to the lid of each can.

44. Door-to-Door Carnation Giveaway
Carnations are affordable, and everyone likes them. This giveaway project can be done anytime, but Mother's Day is a particularly good excuse.

45. Tulip Bulbs
A handful of tulip bulbs is very affordable. When they come up in years to come, that person will reflect on your act of generosity.

46. Potted Plant Giveaways
Marigolds and impatiens can be purchased affordably in numbers. Mums are great in the fall. Small poinsettias are a great touch at Christmas.

47. Flower Seed Packet Giveaways
Give out flower seeds to celebrate spring. Some companies offer the option of printing your church name on the outside of the packet.

48. Weed Spraying
Spray for weeds in cracks in the sidewalk and areas where weeds thrive. Wear rubber gloves.

APPENDIX 1

49. Tree Limb Trimming
Purchase an extending trimmer with a saw and pulley clipper. Beware of electric lines. Before trimming any limbs, get approval from the homeowner.

50. Fireplace Kindling
Bundle up scrap wood and give it out in the fall. Attach your connection message on the binding.

51. School Supplies
Distribute school supplies house-to-house, especially in needy neighborhoods whose residents include many children.

52. Fruit Giveaway
People really like fresh fruit, and they will readily take it. This one goes over great guns across the U.S. An orange, an apple, and a banana along with a connection card in a clear plastic bag is enough. This also works well door-to-door.

53. Sunday Morning Paper Giveaway
Purchase a number of Sunday papers and visit your neighbors. Look for the houses that don't have a paper in the driveway, but be sure you don't knock on the door too early!

PETS

54. Doggie Treats
People often love their pets like family members. Either make from scratch a great doggie treat, or buy them from a pet shop (many shops now offer high-end treats for pets). Wrap several with a ribbon and a connection card and give them out at parks or dog runs.

55. Doggie Dirt Cleanup
It's an unsavory job, but someone has to do it. Jesus said, "If you want to be great in God's kingdom, be the servant of all." Actually, it's not that tough with the right equipment—you can find specialized scooper equipment at a local pet store. Give a connection card to pet owners and park officials in the area.

56. Doggie Wash
This is a great outreach opportunity for kids. Go through a park or your local neighborhood looking for dogs and their owners. Use a vet recommended dog shampoo sold in pet stores.

EVENTS

57. Car Wash
This is an effective, practical service. We offer a car wash every week in the summer. Have a professionally made banner or sign that says "Totally Free Car Wash!" or "Free—No Kidding—Car Wash!" Have a few extroverted, friendly people cheerfully yell at cars driving by, "Free Car Wash!"

58. Single Moms' Oil Change
This is a great stand-alone project for a Sunday morning in the church

APPENDIX 1

parking lot. We provide this service strictly to single moms, though not necessarily just those in our church. This will require a team of folks with knowledge of auto maintenance basics. There are hundreds of sizes of auto filters, so get sign-ups before the event.

59. Bulb Replacement
Set up a station in the corner of a shopping center parking lot. Use a sign that reads, "Free Light Bulb Exam and Replacement." There are only a few common bulb types used in domestic and foreign cars; have an assortment of these available. With just a few basic tools (screwdrivers), just about anyone can pull this one off. Don't use powered screwdrivers— they are more likely to break lens covers.

60. Vegi-Hot Dog Grilling
Like 'em or not, grilled hot dogs bring everyone together. Even when you provide the dogs, buns, and condiments, this is an affordable outreach. Put up a banner that reads, "Free Vegi-Dogs." An excellent opportunity to share about a healthier diet.

61. Clowns
Bring a team of clowns to hand out candy or balloons. This adds fun and excitement to the atmosphere of sharing God's love.

62. Memorial Services for the Un-churched
We have begun to do gratis memorial services for the families of the un-churched. As you reach out to the community with this kind of love and support, you will increasingly find that those you serve will consider you their church, even though they are hardly connected with you.

63. Food Delivery to Shut-ins
Find legitimate shut-ins in your neighborhood. This is a great outreach opportunity for pre-Christians in your church; they are often interested in helping others even though they don't yet know Christ, and a project like this could easily be an entry point to their hearts.

WINTER & CHRISTMAS

64. Snow Shoveling
Men's groups take on their neighborhoods with snow shovels and snow blowers and go door-to-door explaining the project. The snow blowers aren't necessary but very helpful. Most drives and sidewalks can be finished in a matter of minutes. Be sure to bring a hot drink for the workers and neighbors who stop by to watch.

65. Windshield Ice Scraping at Apartment Complexes
Scrape first, ask questions later. Place a connection card on the clean windshield when finished.

66. Windshield Ice Scrapers
Scrapers last a year or less, so early in the season most drivers need another one. Imprint scrapers with your church name, or attach a sticker with your message on it, and leave them on car windshields.

APPENDIX 1

67. Retrieving Cars Stuck in Snow
On heavy snow days, send out teams with four-wheel drive trucks. Using chains and other safety equipment, pull the cars out. Carry a hot drink to warm up those you help. A cell phone is helpful if you need to call for reinforcements.

68. Christmas Gift Wrapping
Wrap Christmas presents for free for mall shoppers. Depending on your mall, you may have to rent the space, purchase the materials, and do it at the hours they ask. On the other hand, some malls give free space, provide the materials and are very accommodating regarding wrapping hours. You aren't in competition with the fancy department stores—they do a classy job, but you can help those in a hurry, those with few or small gifts, or those who just can't afford to spend money on fancy wrapping.

69. Package Check-In
Shoppers are terribly burdened at Christmas. Set up a booth at the mall with a package checking system, and watch over their packages until they're finished shopping. You will be able to talk with them when they drop off their packages and when they return.

70. Gifts at the Mall
Have some small gifts and give away with connection cards.

71. Scotch Tape
Who doesn't need Scotch tape at Christmas? This has been one of our most popular giveaways—it definitely is a practical way to show God's love.

72. Caroling and Candy Canes
Organize a caroling group and go house-to-house in neighborhoods. Take candy canes or a small gift to give, as well. For another spin, go with low income areas, especially inner-city urban ones, and take hot chocolate and cookies and serve the residents.

73. House-to-House Poinsettias
Take small poinsettia plants as "house-to-house" gifts.

74. Tree Giveaway
A few days before Christmas, lot owners are willing to give the trees away. With pickup trucks, deliver them to financially stretched single parent families.

OTHER HOLIDAYS

75. Candy Giveaway
Give out chocolate hearts for Valentine's Day in busy downtown areas or in front of stores. This is an excellent way to do a "giveaway." Rather than ask "Would you like..." say, "Happy Valentine's Day!" and give them a heart and a connection card. You will get very few rejections.

76. Roses
Hand out roses or carnations in busy downtown areas or in front of busy stores. Even men find this appealing, because they can give them away!

Hand a flower and a connection card.

77. Butterfly Cocoons
You can actually buy butterfly cocoons online; it's even possible to purchase cocoons that can be timed to hatch on a given day—within a day or so, anyway. This project is best designed for churches in mild climates.

78. Independence Day Giveaways
Blow-pops and gum balls are a big hit for the Fourth of July. Small American flags are also popular. After dark, glow-in-the-dark sticks are really effective.

79. NOT Halloween
Although we do not endorse this holiday, we can use this event to connect with pre-Christians in ways they can understand. Have a Harvest Festival, an option to the Halloween emphasis that is all around.

COLLEGE CAMPUS OUTREACH

80. Trash Pick-up for Students near Campuses
Start visiting local apartment complexes where students live, asking residents if you can take their garbage out for them. The first time you may get a not-so-good response, but over time people will recognize you and will trust you more. Consider visiting on Sunday afternoons when they are waking up from their Saturday nights with a ton of trash.

81. Bike Fix-up
Many students ride bicycles to class. They often need tune-ups, including tightening brakes, aligning gears, and greasing ball-bearings. Setting up shop can save students money and provide an opportunity to get to know them.

82. Post Cards and Stamps
College students do actually write home on occasion. Provide postcards complete with postage with a sticker that reads, "It's good to write your mom!" Include your connection card.

83. Photocopying
Purchase photocopying coupons at a reduced rate at a local copy center near the college campus. The price shouldn't be more than about five cents per copy. Give these punch cards out on campus. Place church logo and phone number on the card.

84. Breakfast Protein Bars
Healthy, popular among students. Students will take them to eat later, even if they've already had breakfast.

85. Test Essay Booklets and Answer Sheets
Many professors require that exams be done on particular testing materials that the students must purchase themselves. These can include testing booklets, scan-friendly answer sheets, and #2 pencils. They aren't expensive, but they are necessary (particularly around midterms and finals) and readily available at campus bookstores. Purchase them in large numbers at a discount and distribute them with an attached connection

APPENDIX 1

card.

86. Drinks During Late-Night Study Sessions
A little TLC goes a long way. Build a cart that can be wheeled around from dorms to libraries to study areas. This one will have to be manned by non-students.

87. Pizza on Move-In Day at the Dorms
If you want to get the attention of an entire dorm, give away pizza. You will hardly need signs—the aroma will do all the marketing you need. Negotiate a discount with the pizza restaurant for large volumes, or the vendor may be willing to give you the pizza in return for an endorsement.

88. Care Package
Prepare and give away care packages for an entire dorm. Include items like packages of hot chocolate, microwave popcorn, cookies, mints, and gum. The total cost will be much less than a dollar apiece. These can be distributed through student mailboxes or a box in the lobby. Make sure to get permission from the dorm first.

89. Coins for Laundry
These make great giveaways. They usually need to wash clothes.

RADICAL SERVICE IDEAS

90. Dollar Drop
At local malls where any sort of programmatic evangelism is not allowed, this is a way to get the attention of many people very quickly. We take a dollar bill and attach a connection card explaining our project (use removable adhesive). Then we go to a shopping mall and nonchalantly drop dollar bills on the ground.

91. Quarter Drop
Do you know people who can't walk past a vending machine without checking the coin-return? Here's an outreach just for those folks! We place a sticker on one side of the quarter and place these loaded quarters in coin-returns of vending machines of various sorts. This one also works by just placing the coin on the ground or on a bench. Note: Make sure the sticker is larger than the quarter. There are some folks out there who will leave the sticker on the quarter and try to insert it into the phone or vending machine—then you'll get a call from a repairman!

92. Buy Down Gas to Bargain Price
Instead of paying the dollar-plus price, buy down the price to a remarkable rate for a couple of hours and pay the difference to the station owner.

93. Purchasing Meals at the Food Court
Approach one of the managers of a fast-food restaurant or a food court stand and offer, "We'd like to pay the bill for as many customers as this amount of money will pay for."

APPENDIX 1

THINGS TO DO AROUND YOUR CHURCH

94. Pop-Corn Giveaway
Attach a connection card to a bag of popcorn and hand out in the neighborhood next to the church.

95. Rose Giveaway
Go to the houses in Valentine's Day or Mother's Day and give a rose to all the mothers in the neighborhood.

96. Free Oil Changes
Good for a Sunday morning. Advertise around with flyers.

97. Free Haircuts
Make sure you have someone that can cut hair, not one who does that as a hobby.

98. CD for Free
Make a copy of a short presentation on the family, finances or parenting and give away.

99. Use your Kids
Consider having the pathfinders/youth walk through the neighborhood picking up trash and handing out candy. Use a connection card.

100. Home Remodeling
Pick a home in your community that needs TLC and dedicate one day to renovating, landscaping, painting.

101. Block Party
Giveaways, music, good food and a low risk approach to invite the neighborhood. This works good right before classes, where you can give out school supplies.

Steve Sjogren wrote Conspiracy of Kindness, has gained attention across a broad base of church leaders as an effective and creative approach to sharing the love of Christ.

PART II

SMALL GROUP LESSONS

PART II

LESSON 1

THE NEED TO SERVE

SEE

Christ's method alone will give true success in reaching the people. The Savior mingled with men as one who desired their good. He showed His sympathy for them, ministered to their needs, and won their confidence. Then He bade them, 'Follow Me'" Ministry of Healing, 143.

OPEN

1 What kind of attitude should we have toward others, even if they are different? Leviticus 19: 18.
2. Whom should Christians give special attention to?
a. Widows and _____ James 1: 27
b. With _____ Leviticus 19: 34
c. With _____ Isaiah 58: 10
3. Why should we help immigrants/foreigners? Exodus 23: 9.
4. How are we truly different from people who are not believers? Matthew 5: 46-48.
5. What does Jesus do with barriers of race, gender, or social class? Galatians 3:28.

SEND

1. We are brothers. White and Black, Hispanic and North American; rich and poor, we are all brothers and sisters. Man makes distinctions and has created barriers, but when we come to Jesus, these barriers are broken and we look at each other as brothers. How can we (as a group), integrate new people who visit us, so they feel part of us?
2. We all have a responsibility. God is clear about our responsibility toward the less fortunate. The Bible teaches this in text after text-about how to treat people who have no resources or opportunities, especially the immigrant. More than 30 verses in the Bible specify that we should give special attention to the "alien." What can you do with your small group to help people who are immigrants in your community? Don't just talk about it, do it!
3. We all can love, even those who do not love us. We have seen in the study today that we are all brothers. Sometimes other people will not accept our help or our love. The temptation at that time is to forget about them. Do not do so! Continue to love; continue to support; continue to help everyone! This is how we show true Christianity.

Conclusion

The purpose of the following lessons is to help you put your faith into action and get involved in your community's needs. Discuss as a group a service project to the community and develop it together this month. Let's make it happen!

LESSON 2
THE TIME TO SERVE

PART II 2

SEARCH

"There is a time for everything, and a season for every activity under heaven. I know that there is nothing better for men than to be happy and **do good** while they live" Ecclesiastes 3:12.

OPEN

1. Look at the text above for a moment (Ecclesiastes 13:12). It mentions two important things. One is to be happy, and the other one is to do good. Are they related? How?
2. Before you make a schedule and plan out your activities, what essential component should be considered? James 4:13-15.
3. Sometimes we are so caught up in our religious activities that we fail to serve the people that need it most (Read Luke 10:31-32). Do you see that happening in your church? What can you do to change it?
4. What clear instruction do we have regarding our time management? Ephesians 5:16.
5. If we consistently dedicate time to serve and minister to others, what will happen? Galatians 6:9.

SEND

There are three ways to manage your time in such a way that you can serve others.
1. Slow down. In a recent study, 50 percent surveyed said they "want to slow down, but don't know how." How do you slow down? One way is to realize that you will never finish everything you have to do. Never! So slow down today, notice the needs of people around you. How can we practice this? How do you slow down?
2. Seek God. As you slow down, make sure you include intentional times of prayer and reading of the Word, as well as times for fasting. Ask God to reveal to you hurting people that surround you, and when He does, minister to them. What's the best time of day for you to connect with God?
3. Set goals. Author Brian Tracy says that for every minute you spend planning the day before, you save 10 minutes the next day. How clear are your goals? What specific goals do you have for serving others this year? This week? This decade?

Conclusion
The purpose of this lesson is to help you slow down, so you can put your faith into action and get involved in your community. Discuss as a group how your service project is going. Make it happen!

LESSON 3
LIFE IS NOT SELF-SERVICE

SEE
Therefore I tell you, do not worry about your life, what you will eat or drink; or about your body, what you will wear. Is not life more important than food, and the body more important than clothes? 26 Look at the birds of the air; they do not sow or reap or store away in barns, and yet your heavenly Father feeds them. Are you not much more valuable than they? 27 Can any one of you by worrying add a single hour to your life? Matthew 6:25-27 (emphasis supplied).

OPEN
1. Look at the verses above. Notice how many times God says the word "you." His objective is for you to focus on Him and others, and not on yourself. Is that hard for you?
2. This next text is very provocative. Read Philippians 2:3. The last part says we should consider others as superior to ourselves. Isn't that dangerous for our self-esteem? What is the Bible trying to teach us?
3. What is wrong with an attitude of me-first, you-never? Luke 12:18-20.
4. When we focus on others, who really are we serving? Matthew 25:34-36.
5. The phrase "one another" appears several times in Scripture. What can we do to one another? John 13:35.

SEND
There are three things you can do to take your eyes off yourself and focus instead on others.
1. Interruptions. If you think about it, many of Jesus' miracles were done when He was on his way to do something else. He was being interrupted! Welcome interruptions, especially when they are in the form of a person needing help. How do you react when interrupted, really? How can you improve that response?
2. Invitations. Invite people to share your life. No man is an island. Jesus told His disciples to go and invite people to a banquet. God has given you the opportunity to have a banquet of blessings. Whom will you invite to share those blessings?
3. Imitation. Look to the example of Jesus. Imitate His strategy. The best description of that strategy is found in a book called Ministry of Healing. In it Ellen White writes, "Christ's method alone will give true success in reaching the people. The Savior mingled with men as one who desired their good. He showed His sympathy for them, ministered to their needs, and won their confidence. Then He bade them, 'Follow Me'" page 143. With whom are you connecting? For whom are you showing sympathy?

Conclusion
The purpose of this lesson is to help you to look to the needs of others, not as an interruption, but as a welcome part of your life. Discuss as a group how your service project is going. Make it happen!

LESSON 4

THE COST OF SERVICE

SEE
"Give, and it will be given to you. A good measure, pressed down, shaken together and running over, will be poured into your lap. For with the measure you use, it will be measured to you" Luke 6:38.

OPEN
1. In the story of the Good Samaritan, what did the Samaritan do besides giving mere moral support to the wounded traveler? Luke 10:33-35.
2. How does God feel about people who just say, "I'll pray for you," when they see a need? James 2:15-17.
3. What happens when people give God what little they have? John 6:9-11.
4. Read the following line: "Giving is not giving unless it interrupts your lifestyle." Reflect on this for a moment. Is your giving following this guideline?
5. How is the principle of giving best illustrated? Philippians 2:5-7.

SEND
There are three things you can do, to combat the monster of materialism in your life.
1. Give. In a world of selfishness, where people look for first for their own benefit, God turns materialism on its ugly head and says simply: "Give." Four powerful letters. Have the freedom to give. What material possession would you give up if asked? Which one would you rather walk over hot coals than give up?
2. Give first. Are people "broke" because they do not give, or are they not able to give because they are "broke"? That is an important question, sort of like, "What came first, the chicken or the egg?" Our central text for today answers it unequivocally. Take the first step. Give first. People have it all wrong. They wait on the Lord, then give. That is backwards! Give, then wait on the Lord. He'll come through.
3. Give expectantly. Look at the text for today. In just two lines it mentions the word "will" three times. It will be given to you. It will be poured in your lap. It will be measured to you. We don't give because we want something in return, yet we can give with confidence that God will take care of us. What are you trusting God to do this week in your finances? What do you need Him to do right now?

Conclusion
The purpose of this lesson is to help you to understand the blessing that giving brings to both the giver and the receiver. Discuss as a group how your service project is going. Make it happen!

PART II — 5

LESSON 5

OPEN HAND CHRISTIANS

SEE

Serving means giving. Today's lesson deals with the importance of maintaining an open hand: to receive from God and to give to others.

"He who did not spare his own son, but gave him up for us all—how will he not also, along with him, graciously give us all things," Romans 8:32.

"Generosity is the spirit of heaven. The all-encompassing love of Christ was revealed on the cross. he gave all he had, and he gave himself, so man could be saved. The cross of Christ is a call go generosity for every disciple of the Savior. The principle it proclaims is to give, always give," *Counsels on Stewardship*, p. 16.

OPEN

1. As he describes the moral condition of humanity in the last days, what characteristics opposed to the principle of giving does Paul point out? 2 Timothy 3:2

___

2. In a world plagued with selfishness, what does Jesus want His disciples to do for the less fortunate? Proverbs 14:31; 19:17; Acts 20:35

___

3. In a world where money is a God, what act of worship and recognition does Jesus ask of His disciples? Malachi 3:10, 11; Luke 11:42; 2 Corinthians 9:6, 7

___

4. Why does King David say we should give? 1 Chronicles 29:14

___

5. There are different motives why we should give. Mark any of the following that you consider to be taught in the Bible.

❑ **Because God needs what I have.**

LESSON 5

- ❏ Because if I don't give, I will not receive.
- ❏ Because giving is a blessing.
- ❏ Because God wants me to represent Him in a selfish world.
- ❏ Because God asks it of us.
- ❏ Because it helps me fight selfishness.
- ❏ Because someday I will need someone to give to me.
- ❏ Because in giving, I worship God.

SEND

1. Apply the principle of the open hand. The open hand is able to receive, and while it remains open, it can also give. When the hand closes to grasp all that it has received and no longer gives, it generally stops receiving. Do you know someone who is passing through a time of need?

2. God invites you to give because He already gave to you. In reality, when we give, we're only *transferring* what God has given us already. We are administrators of the funds through which Jesus wants us to *represent* Him to the rest of the world. If you apply this principle, you can help the needy person answer this question, "Where is God when I'm needy?" Also, when God asks you to return the tithe and to give offerings, you are only becoming a means to *channel* His money to benefit the cause of God (humanity).

3. We don't give in order to receive. As we apply this principle of Heaven; God gives us more, because He knows we can be a greater blessing for others. Jesus knows that letting go of money is not easy for our sinful nature; that's why He has promised to open the windows of Heaven to supply our real needs, spiritual as well as material. This is why the Bible assures us in the key text: If He is able to give His only Son; will He not be able to give us? With Him, all things are possible.

Conclusion

Worship the Lord by returning tithe and offerings. If you have never done so, test it today. You will see that the Lord is good and it will help your church to make a greater impact both locally and around the world.

The idea behind this resource is to motivate, educate and release members to be the hands and feet of Jesus in our communities through a 40 Day Season of Service (SOS).

Daily Lesson:
Each lesson contains three parts:
See It- we always start with scripture. Don't be too quick to skip over it. Read it. Read it again. Internalize it. Believe it. Share it.
Obey It- This part shares a few principles to learn. They usually relate to the verse you just read. They are short, practical and biblical.
Share It- The last part of the lesson is where you turn your knowledge about service into action. Most of us are educated well above our level of obedience, so if you are only reading and not serving, this resource will be only partially successful. Each day you will have **3 options** of service activities for you to do **THAT** day. Pick one. (or more) There is also a list of **100 more** service projects that you, your church or small group can do during the SOS and beyond at the end of the book in **APPENDIX 1**.

Small Group Study
Included in this resource there are five small group lessons, enough for **one per week** for 40 days. These lessons can be studied in homes, workplaces, during Sabbath Services, or wherever God leads you. They are simple, easy and very practical.

Chronology
Start Day- first step is to start. It works best on a weekend day, but you can start it any day.
Daily 40- the next step is to complete the daily devotional/action step. If you miss a day, just go on to the next one. Chose "done" over "perfect."
Big Serve Weekend- Usually in the middle of the 40 days, there is a weekend that is reserved for larger projects. Check with your local leadership for dates.
Service Celebration- The last step is the final day of the 40 days. That Sabbath the ideal is that local civic leaders be invited and honored at the local church as well as informed about what the church has been doing. It's a high day!

NOTES